Pictorial Guide to

The
Quaker
Tapestry

Research into the subject matter for the panels and for the text of the 1989 *Guide* was undertaken by Harold Nichols, Betty Harris, and many of the groups concerned, with contributions also from David Butler, Elfrida Vipont Foulds, Ormerod Greenwood and Anne Wynn-Wilson, and edited by Margaret Simpson. Revisions for the 1992 *Guide in colour* were the responsibility of Kathleen Cottrell, Edward Milligan and Margaret Simpson. The text, completely revised for the current *Pictorial guide*, has been prepared by Edward Milligan under the direction of the Publications Committee of the Quaker Tapestry at Kendal. All of the panels were photographed for this book by Bryn Lennon Photography.

ISBN 0 9525433 1 1

Designed by Jeremy Greenwood,
Woodbridge, cover design by Phil Cousins,
P R Design, Barrow-in-Furness, and printed by
Middletons of Ambleside, Compston Road,
Ambleside, Cumbria LA22 9DJ

for The Quaker Tapestry at Kendal
Friends Meeting House, Stramongate
Kendal, Cumbria LA9 4BH

Table of contents

The order of the panels requires some explanation. The Introduction tells how the Yearly Meeting of Quakers in Britain has periodically revised a book of collected counsel to its members. When the Tapestry began, the text used was that of 1959 published as *Christian faith and practice in the experience of the Society of Friends*: the Tapestry panels were arranged using its chapter headings as a basis (see appendix B). Yearly Meeting 1994 approved a further revision entitled *Quaker faith and practice*, the chapter arrangement and much of the content understandably being different. This explanation may help to clarify the arrangement of the *Pictorial Guide* and some of the headings adopted.

The panels were designed and embroidered by the individuals or groups mentioned at the end of the descriptive text for each panel: very many embroiderers who gave invaluable help joined a group at a distance from their home and space does not permit their detailed mention. The panels show what a very great deal the Tapestry owes to children's research, drawing, design and embroidery. Children have been an essential part of the group and their work is not separately mentioned except that of the Taunton children, who have a special place in the Tapestry's history, and one or two other cases of particular significance. Supervision of the embroidery was by Anne Wynn-Wilson, Ann Castle, Ann Nichols, Jill Robinson and Cathy Spence, and, at the beginning of the project, by Maggie Goodrich.

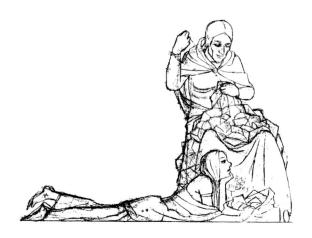

By the needle you shall draw the thread, and by that which is
past see how that which is to come will be drawne on.
George Herbert, 'Outlandish proverbs', 1640

To those who look and listen, a thing well made
causes the past to call to the future.
Haida chief from British Columbia

Introduction

How did the idea of a Quaker Tapestry come about? When did it all happen? Who was involved in the vision, the design, the embroidery? What story or message is it trying to tell? Where was it exhibited and where can it be seen today?

This is not the place to attempt a detailed answer to all these questions, for that is done elsewhere. It is sufficient to say that the 77 panels of the Quaker Tapestry came into being as a result of a chance remark by an eleven-year-old boy attending the children's class of a small Quaker meeting in the south-west of England in 1981. His teacher, to whom the remark was made, was Anne Wynn-Wilson, who was an accomplished embroiderer. She had the vision of a number of large tapestry panels telling something of the Quaker story and beliefs. In August 1982 she mounted an exhibition at the yearly meeting of British Quakers, held that year at the University of Warwick, and included the first completed tapestry panel. Her idea and determination aroused an enthusiastic response from many Friends and some 400 suggestions for panel subjects were received. This number was carefully reduced to a manageable 60 but eventually rose to 77. Designers came forward, embroidery groups were formed, training workshops were arranged and even Tapestry holidays were organised, all of which helped to foster the idea that this was truly a community endeavour. Altogether, more than 4,000 men, women and children in fifteen countries have 'had a hand' in the creation of the Quaker Tapestry.

The Tapestry has been described as a celebration of Quaker experience and insights, though Friends would hasten to add that Quakers do not by any means lay sole claim to them. Quakerism arose out of the political and religious ferment of the mid-17th century. Friends met (and meet) for worship in gathered stillness without priest or other appointed leader, words of ministry or of prayer being given by any one of the worshippers, man or woman or, indeed, child. Friends' belief in 'that of God in every one' enabled them to conceive of a universal church comprehending (in the words of Robert Barclay, an early Scots Friend) 'all, of whatsoever nation, kindred, tongue or people, though remote from those who profess Christ and Christianity in words, as become obedient to the holy light, the testimony of God in their hearts'.

Business meetings, like meetings for worship, were conducted without an authority figure bearing a title such as president or chairman, for Quakers saw the power of God alone as their authority. Thus the Friend asked to record their decisons was simply termed 'clerk'. A system of area monthly meetings was established, with county (later regional) quarterly meetings, and a national yearly meeting – Britain

yearly meeting is (1997) one of some 40 yearly meetings worldwide. The responsibility for embroidering a panel varied from a local group to an area monthly meeting as is revealed in the title names.

Quakers believe that religion applies to the whole of life, that inward and outward, sacred and secular are inseparably related: thus there grew up corporately accepted standards of behaviour. The Quaker testimonies – against war, or oaths, or tithes – were a witness to a lifestyle consistent with standards of simplicity, integrity and respect for human personality. On many day-to-day problems, local Quaker meetings in Britain sought advice of the national yearly meeting: its responses year by year were in 1738 collected as *Christian and brotherly advices*. Since then, Friends in Britain have revised their book of collected counsel nearly every generation: the last two revisions are referred to on page 3.

The panels have been displayed in many exhibitions, both in the British Isles and beyond seas – Aberdeen Art Gallery; the Royal Festival Hall, London; Bayeux; Lincoln Cathedral; the Royal Hibernian Society, Dublin; Winchester Cathedral. In April 1994 the permanent Quaker Tapestry Exhibition Centre opened in the impressive Georgian meeting house in Kendal. A set of full-size photographic reproductions has been made for exhibitions elsewhere and the experience and message of the Tapestry is further available through many publications, meetings, and embroidery workshops. This book is intended to help those who have already seen the panels to relive the experience and those who have not yet had the opportunity to gain some measure of the experience. The text has been reduced to the minimum needed for explaining the significance of each panel. Biographical notes have been provided for those who wish to discover a little more: where no biographical note is provided, years of birth and death are, where possible, given in the descriptive notes to the panel.

But enough of this introduction – now for the panels.

Quaker Tapestry
Publications Committee

The prism

George Fox in 1648 saw 'how that every man was enlightened by the divine light of Christ; and I saw it shine through all'. It was this insistence that the light was universal that contemporaries found so scandalous. But Quakers cited John 1:9 ('that was the true light, which lighteth every man that cometh into the world') to the point where it became known as 'the Quakers' text'. It was not that they denied, or even belittled, the powers of sin and darkness, but they insisted that looking at the darkness, 'crying up sin', was merely negative, whereas looking at the light not only showed people their darkness but gave them the power to overcome it. Early Quakers also taught that the light leads to unity – not to outward uniformity but to a deeper unity in the spirit. Thus Isaac Penington wrote in 1659, 'this is the true ground of love and unity, not that a man walks and does just as I do , but because I feel the same Spirit and life in him'. The prism, therefore, is a symbol of the richness of this unity in diversity. The context of the quotation in this panel is important, for the sentence is not an assertion about the Society of Friends, save as an illustration of a general principle. The words come from the preamble to a chapter of *Christian faith and practice* entitled 'Spiritual experiences of Friends': the previous sentence recalls how such a chapter was 'first conceived in 1921, after a time of theological difference, by Friends who longed not to be separated by dispute, but to share an experience which men and women had reached in diverse ways'. This *Pictorial guide*, like the Tapestry itself, is meant to express the diverse ways in which Quakers, men, women and children, have expressed in word and action the faith that is in them.

Designed and embroidered by Anne Wynn-Wilson, with some embroidery by Winifred Booker

A1 George Fox's convincement

George Fox grew up in Fenny Drayton, *left*, a village with puritan lords of the manor and rectors, *right*, going back to the reign of Elizabeth I. He was apprenticed to a shoemaker, *left*, 'that dealt in wool, and used grazing, and sold cattle; and a great deal went through my hands'. A turning point in his life, *right*, was in 1643: he was 'upon business at a fair [that is, a market]' at Atherstone when his cousin Bradford and a friend 'asked me to drink part of a jug of beer with them, and I, being thirsty, went in with them', only to discover 'when they had drunk a glass apiece' that the occasion threatened to turn into a drunken orgy. Shocked by the failure of professing Christians to live up to the standards they proclaimed, he left home and travelled extensively for four years in search of spiritual help and fellowship. The figures at the foot serve as reminder that these travels were during a time of civil war and political and religious questioning. The experience he describes, *left*, came to him in 1647 'when all my hopes in all men were gone, so that I

had nothing outwardly to help me, nor could tell what to do'. He had shortly before this met Elizabeth Hooton at Mansfield and most of his time in the late 1640s was spent in the east midlands (Derbyshire, Nottinghamshire, Leicestershire): here as elsewhere he encountered many folk who were on a like spiritual journey and his personality, ministry, and great pastoral gifts drew them into an enduring fellowship. These journeys culminated in his arrest at Derby in October 1650 (*panel F1*).

Designed by Anne Wynn-Wilson; embroidered by her and Taunton children

In the embroidered panel:

JAMES NAYLER c1617–1660

There is a Spirit which I feel that delights to do no evil nor to revenge any wrong, but delights to endure all things, in hope to enjoy its own in the end.... If it be betrayed, it bears it, for its ground + spring is the mercies and forgiveness of God. its crown is meekness, its life is everlasting love unfeigned, it takes its kingdom with entreaty + not with contention, keeps it by lowliness of mind... I found it alone, being forsaken

1656 Exeter

Bristol

London

Bridewell 1659

James Nayler (1617?-1660) was a Yorkshireman from West Ardsley, near Wakefield. In 1643 he joined the parliamentary army, fighting at the battle of Dunbar (3 September 1650) and at Worcester, just one year later. He was one of a small group whom Fox visited in the late autumn of 1651, when he was convinced of Quakerism. In the spring of 1652, after Fox had again visited the group, he 'was at the plow, meditating on the things of God', *top left*, when he felt called to leave home and devote himself to spreading the news of his new-found faith. By July 1652 he was at Swarthmoor Hall (*panel C1*). He was soon in the forefront of the new movement, his charismatic personality and powerful preaching winning him golden opinions, especially in London. In 1656, travelling westward to meet Fox, from whom he had become estranged, he was arrested and gaoled at Exeter, *bottom left*. Fox, released from a long imprisonment at Launceston, came to Exeter, but a meeting of the two Quaker leaders did credit to neither. In these tense circumstances and swayed by adulatory followers, Nayler entered Bristol in October 1656 'acting a sign' of Christ's entry into Jerusalem, *bottom, left of centre*. Tried before Parliament for blasphemy, he suffered extreme punishment and three years' imprisonment, *bottom right*. In 1660, reconciled at last with Fox, he set out homeward. Some miles beyond Huntingdon he was robbed and bound and found towards evening in a field, *middle*. He was taken to a Friend's house and his dying words form the text of the panel. The rose, *left*, is a symbol of the love of God, which Nayler poetically expressed in 1659: 'When I was as one altogether helpless, when tribulation and anguish was upon me day and night, as a Father thou was with me'.

Designed and embroidered by the Bristol group

The embroidered panel reads:

MEETING for SUFFERINGS was formed 1675 to record + alleviate the sufferings of Friends

JAMES PARNELL after great suffering died in Colchester Prison 1656 aged nineteen

Be willing that self shall suffer for Truth + not the Truth for self

Yorkshire "I must and I will see George Fox"

Kendal · Cumbria · Dales · Notts · Leeds · Sheffield · Carlisle · Retford

A3   James Parnell; Meeting for Sufferings

James Parnell (1636-1656) of Retford, Nottinghamshire, was 15 years old when, in 1651, he became a convinced Quaker. His determination to see George Fox, then imprisoned at Carlisle, involved him in a hazardous journey, *bottom.* Parnell then preached and worked tirelessly in Cambridge and Essex. Accused of causing a riot, he was imprisoned at Colchester, being put into a high niche in the castle wall, which he could reach only by a ladder six feet too short, and then by climbing a rope. Eventually he was too weak and cold to hold the rope and fell, being gravely injured, *centre.* He was then put in a little low hole where he died in 1656, after eight months of imprisonment. Up to the passing of the Toleration Act 1689 about 15,000 Quakers suffered various legal sentences and over 450 died in prison. Many prosecutions were in fact illegal and Meeting for Sufferings was set up to 'stay the arm of the oppressor' and to co-ordinate what had sometimes been conflicting initiatives by different groups of Friends. As a weekly gathering of London Quakers,

with an effective network of county correspondents, it became a formidable pressure group. If, initially, its efforts were on behalf of Friends themselves, it found its efforts increasingly on behalf of others, as for example the ending of the slave trade (*panel F3*). By the early nineteenth century it was meeting monthly rather than weekly and, as transport improved, country Friends were able to attend its sittings, so that it became a representative gathering of some 200 members. The range of matters brought before it steadily widened – slavery, peace, relief work, unemployment, penal affairs, race relations and much else, besides more domestic Quaker business.

Designed by Joe McCrum; embroidered by the Harrow group

Within the embroidery:
Pressed into the· Royal Prince · Scarborough 1665

RICHARD SELLAR

I am at peace
with God + all men +
with you my adversaries.

I was to die But no man came neither

a mouth opened against me

I am not free to do the Kings work.

Richard Seller   A4

Richard Seller was a longshore fisherman of Kilnsea, at the extreme south of the Yorkshire coast. Little is known of him but he is probably to be identified with the Richard Seller of Easington in Holderness, who married in 1678 the widow Priscilla Camplin (d. 1694), and the Richard Seller of Scarborough, who married in 1696 the widow Ellen Bartindale (d. 1714) of Waxham [Waxholme] in Holderness. In 1665, during the second war with the Dutch, he was pressganged at Scarborough, and was assigned to the flagship of Admiral Sir Edward Spragge. He refused orders on grounds of conscience, *bottom*. He added that he would not live at the king's charge for victuals. Brought before the captain he said that his 'warfare was spiritual, therefore I durst not fight with carnal weapons'. He was brutally beaten and lay in irons for twelve days, but his patient endurance won him friends - the carpenter's mate brought him food secretly, saying 'I have meat of my own which is not at the king's charge'. He was court-martialled and condemned to be hanged. Next morning he was

brought on deck, prepared for execution, and became the central character in a curious scene. After an interchange between the judge and the admiral, the latter three times said (in Seller's words) that 'If any Man or Men on board of the Ship, would come forward and give Evidence, that I had done any Thing that I deserved Death for, I should have it, provided they were credible Persons'. Nobody spoke against him, *right*, and the admiral proclaimed him a free man. It may well be that the whole episode was to frighten him: whether his life had been in serious jeopardy may be doubted, but his own calm courage can never be in doubt.

Designed by Joe McCrum; embroidered by Anne Wynn-Wilson, Mary Siegle and Taunton children

We asked counsel of the **LORD** as the **WOODHOUSE** sailed for the New World ·1657

Cut through · steer a straight course + mind nothing but **ME**

Robert Fowler thou hast her not for nothing

Contrary to my will she was brought to London where eleven Friends awaited a captain willing to take them to America

A5 **The voyage of the *Woodhouse***

In 1657 Robert Fowler, a Quaker master mariner of Bridlington, Yorkshire, was, *left*, building the *Woodhouse* for his own use locally. As he worked on her, he heard an inner voice telling him that the ship was destined for some special service, *words under ship*. This was confirmed when it was freighted and made ready for sea, for, *wording at bottom*, he found himself not at some local port but in London, distraught at being parted from his business, wife and family. He conferred with London Quakers, including George Fox, and came to accept that his small vessel was to convey the 11 Friends, *bottom*, awaiting passage for New England. His troubles were not over, for the pressgang took all his crew except two men and three boys. He put in to Portsmouth where another captain looked askance and said *he* would never venture the Atlantic in a ship so small. Nothing daunted, Fowler was able to augment his depleted crew and set sail. The *Woodhouse* was in convoy with three large ships going to Newfoundland but, seeing a Dutch man-of-war bearing down on them, 'the three great ships were much afraid, and tacked about with what speed they could', leaving the Quakers 'without hope of help as to the outward'. However, the Dutch ship was struck by a contrary wind and Friends, seeking divine guidance as to their course, received it, *middle, wording above ship at top*, and had a sense of 'the Lord leading our vessel even as it were a man leading a horse by the head'. The panel depicts, *above the sails*, the hand of God, a traditional form for expressing his guidance. After a two-month adventurous voyage the frail barque reached Long Island, near New Amsterdam, a tolerant Dutch colony. The small houses, *right*, have as background the skyscrapers of the New York it was to become.

Designed by Anne Wynn-Wilson and drawn by Joe McCrum; embroidered by Ann Nichols and the Nottingham group

The American Quaker John Woolman (1720-1772) in his childhood threw stones at a robin *left* and killed her. Contrite because 'those young ones for which she was so careful must now perish for want of their dam to nourish them' he realised that it would be less cruel to climb the tree and kill them than leave them to slow death. When he was about 36 he gave up a lucrative business in merchandise and took up tailoring (symbolised by the basket) so that he could 'live more free from outward cumbers'. His first journey to the southern states in 1746 brought him face to face with aspects of slavery he had not hitherto met. On his second southern journey in 1757 he felt uneasy at accepting free hospitality from slave-owners and, before leaving, would speak to his hosts, proffering silver to give to their slaves for what they had done: he expressed his concern in such a way that 'few if any manifested any resentment of the offer'. In 1761 he decided to give up wearing dyed clothing, *centre left*, 'dyes being invented partly to please the eye and partly to hide

dirt'. In 1763, *top right*, he journeyed to meet the Indians 'whose ancestors were the owners and possessers of the land where we dwell, and who for a very small consideration assigned their inheritance to us'. In 1772 he felt called to service in England: travelling steerage on the *Mary and Elizabeth, centre right*, he felt great concern for the conditions under which the sailors lived and worked. In England he travelled on foot, *bottom*, avoiding stagecoaches for 'it is common for horses to be killed with hard driving' and postboys 'who ride long stages suffer greatly in winter nights, and at several places I have heard of their being froze to death'. Soon after arriving at York he was taken ill with smallpox and during his dying days was nursed, *bottom left*, in a house just outside the city.

Designed by Wendy Gillett and the York children; embroidered by the York group

A7   **Conscientious objection**

The Society of Friends, the Mennonites, and the Church of the Brethren are known as the historic peace churches. Richard Seller (*panel A4*) was only one of many early Quakers who found themselves in positions where they had to say 'no' on grounds of conscience. Under the Militia Acts of the eighteenth and early nineteenth centuries a number of Friends suffered imprisonment, but it was the Military Service Act 1916 which first affected Friends – and many others – in large numbers. Tribunals were composed, *left*, of local tradesmen and dignitaries, with a military representative. They had to consider claims on grounds of health or hardship as well as conscience, and it is perhaps no wonder that their procedures, attitudes and decisions varied widely from place to place. Exemption might be absolute, conditional or temporary. If a claim were rejected, or if a man could not accept the conditions, he would be sent a calling-up notice, arrested for not responding, and handed over to the military, where he could continue his witness only by disobeying an order. Over 6,000 men, many of them Friends, were arrested in this way, the usual prison sentence, *top right*, being two years. Some belligerent women, *centre*, offered white feathers (symbol of cowardice) to anyone not in uniform. In the second world war the 19 regional tribunals dealt only with conscientious objection and were chaired by county court judges. Up to 1948 over 62,000 men and women appeared before them. Nearly 3,000 were registered unconditionally and over 23,000 conditional on undertaking hospital, forestry or land work, *bottom*, relief work or service with the Friends Ambulance Unit (*panels F7, F8*). Over 17,000 were given the condition of non-combatant service in the forces and over 18,000 were turned down.

Designed by Joe McCrum and Anne Wynn-Wilson; embroidered by Margaretta Playfair and the Cambridge group

In the embroidery:

1895 the **MANCHESTER** conference challenged the old thinking + distressed some

Friends are not bound by a heritage or creeds + need not break with their great past to put themselves in touch with the present.

John Wilhelm Rowntree 1868–1905

"God's truth is given for every age, + it is our duty to welcome the light which may just be reaching us." Frances Thompson. 1840–1920

Money raised for ROMANIA £250

Mum going to AFRICA Conference 1992

Quietist Friends

More Freedom

SPEAKING in MEETING

Mid-nineteenth century British Quakerism was predominantly evangelical. The witness of quietist Friends, who tended to keep to the old plain dress, *bottom left*, had been to dependence on the holy spirit: evangelicals accused them of mysticism and theological vagueness; they, in turn, accused evangelicals of advocating 'mere head knowledge' and '*creaturely* activity' – for quietists could be active enough once assured that the activity was divinely inspired. In general, Quakers were, like most of their fellow-Christians, disturbed by Darwin's *On the origin of species* (1859) and by the textual criticism of the Bible following Tischendorf's discovery of Codex Siniaticus the same year. Fresh (not altogether welcome) thinking came to Friends with the publication of *A reasonable faith* (1884) and *The gospel of divine help* (1887). At the 1893 yearly meeting of British Quakers the 25-year-old John Wilhelm Rowntree complained that much of the ministry in meetings for worship was in a language alien to the younger generation. In 1895 a national conference at

Manchester meeting house, *centre and panel C4*, attracted 1,300 Friends for three days to listen to 30 papers, seven of them by women, covering a wide range of subjects including attitudes to social questions and 'modern thought'. The conference brought together the best in the quietist and evangelical traditions, relating both to a new, more liberal, outlook: it led directly to the summer school movement and the foundation of Woodbrooke (*panel B6*). The Rover safety bicycle (1885), *bottom, left of centre*, had led to greater freedom and mobility (*panel C9*); the decade also heralded twentieth century concerns, *bottom, centre to right*, for relief work, a more widely-shared vocal ministry, and increased international awareness.

Designed by Anne Wynn-Wilson and Wendy Gillett; embroidered at the Quaker Tapestry Exhibition Centre at Kendal

"SWEAR NOT AT ALL" matthew chapter 5 v34

The ability to claim Burgess Rights regained Aberdeen 1714

Friend Robert Barclay reading the Act of the Privy Council.

We regard the taking of oaths as contrary to the teaching of Christ, as setting up a double standard of truthfulness, whereas sincerity and truth should be practised in all dealings of life   Christian Faith & Practice 1911 + 25

A9 Oaths

In the seventeenth century the oath was commonplace for a whole host of everyday transactions as well as more important matters. Those who could not swear were barred from carrying on trade in corporate towns, proving wills involving goods or chattels, giving evidence to defend title to land, or entering many of the professions or positions of office. Quakers refused to swear, quoting scripture in support of their position. Their objection was, however, more fundamental. Truth (*panel B4*) implied the need always to speak the truth, not merely when under oath. William Penn (*panels F2, F11*) wrote in 1675: 'People swear to the end that they may speak truth; Christ would have them speak truth to the end that they might not swear'. After the Restoration it became easy to convict a Quaker, if all else failed, by tendering the oath of allegiance, since, though asserting their loyalty, they would not swear. On lesser matters those who administered oaths (in the proving of wills for example) often turned a blind eye when faced with Quaker scruples. Relief for Friends in England & Wales was obtained through the Affirmation Acts 1696, 1722; but it was not until the Oaths Act 1888 that affirmation became possible for all. In Scotland the affirmation as an alternative to the oath was a well-established tradition. Burgess oaths, however, presented problems, as at Aberdeen where the provost and baillies inserted a clause in the oath designed to exclude Catholics and Quakers. Friends, unwilling to compromise or lose their rights, campaigned energetically and in 1714 received a ruling from the lord advocate that a solemn affirmation was sufficient, and an act of the Privy Council ordered that the offending words be removed from that burgess oath. Robert Barclay II is seen, *right*, presenting this act to the town council.

Designed by Avril Brown; embroidered by Friends in Scotland

Within the embroidery:
SEDBERGH · FIRBANK FELL
PRESTON PATRICK · BRIGFLATTS · 1652

Many groups of Seekers   heard George Fox preach

Keep your feet upon the top of the mountain and sound deep to that of God in everyone.

Firbank Fell: George Fox preaching B1

After journeying through the east midlands and southern and eastern Yorkshire George Fox in 1652 was travelling towards the north-west. On Pendle Hill (*panel D1*) he had a vision of 'a great people to be gathered' and these he found in the neighbourhood of Sedbergh and Preston Patrick. On Wednesday 9 June he 'got up by a tree' outside Sedbergh church, *left*, at the time of the hiring fair and 'declared the everlasting truth' for several hours. A captain asked why he would not go into the church as a fit place to preach in, but Fox 'opened to the people that the ground and house was no holier than another place, and that the house was not the church, but the people which Christ is the head of'. On the following Sunday he preached for some three hours to a thousand people on nearby Firbank Fell. Many worshippers looked out from the chapel nearby 'and thought it a strange thing to see a man preach on a hill or mountain and not in their church (as they called it)'. But Fox declared that 'Christ was come, who ended the temple, and the priests, and the tithes'. The figure of Fox, *centre*, represents him not only on Firbank Fell but also on Pendle Hill where 'when I came atop of it I saw Lancashire sea' or, as we would now say, Morecambe Bay. On Wednesday 16 June he was at Preston Patrick chapel where there was a meeting of the seekers once a month – people coming from as far as Lancaster and Yealand, from Underbarrow and Grayrigg. Fox sat near the door and for half an hour there was silence: the preacher 'seemed uneasey, and pulled out his bible & opened it, & stood up severall times, sitting downe againe and Closeing his Booke'. Fox finally preached with power – 'A nottable day Indeede never to be forgotten by me, Thomas Camm I being then present A schoole boy but aboute 12 years of age'.

Designed and embroidered by Anne Wynn-Wilson

The embroidery contains the following text:

1623 MARY FISHER 1698

one of the many women "publishers of the truth"

the world, East + West, was their Parish

1657

for God's Spirit dwelt in every man

1652 ELIZ HOOTON · YORK GAOL

CAMBRIDGE MARKET 1653

1655 · OLD ANNE AUSTIN

BOSTON MASS · MARY DYER 1660

B2 Mary Fisher

Women played a substantial and important part in spreading the Quaker message and the service and sufferings of a few of them (*see biographical notes*) are depicted here, *bottom*. Mary Fisher is best known for her visit in 1657-8 to the Great Turk. In the spring of 1657 a group of six Friends, three men and three women, *left*, set out towards the middle east. By the end of July they had reached Leghorn, where besides preaching they distributed books in English, French and Latin. On 20 August they left for Zante (Zakinthos), arriving on 6 September. Here the group divided, two going across the Morea to Corinth and Athens, while Mary Fisher and three others reached Smyrna (Izmir) in mid-November, the others joining them at the very end of the year. The English consul, hearing of their proposed visit to the Sultan, was kind but encouraged them to return home. They took ship for Venice but a strong wind drove them again to Zante. Here, again, the group divided – Mary Fisher and Beatrice Beckley undertaking 'to passe into the Morea againe into

Turkey to goe toward Adrianople, where we heare the Turkes Emperour lyes with his Army'. They arrived there in May or early June 1658. When Sultan Mohammed IV, a young man of 17, was told that an Englishwoman had come with a message from the great God, he caused her to be received with state ceremony. She was now aged 35 and stood silent before him, waiting for God's guidance, speaking then through an interpreter, *right*. The Sultan said he had understood every word and it was the truth and she 'departed the camp to Constantinople, without a guard, whither she came without the least hurt or scoff'.

Designed by Margery Levy; embroidered by the Southampton group

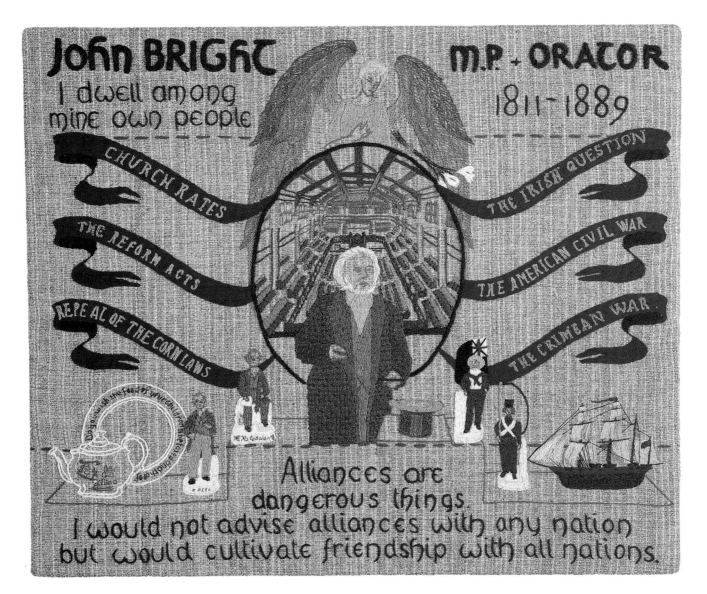

Within the embroidered panel:

John BRIGHT   **M.P - ORATOR**

I dwell among mine own people   1811 - 1889

CHURCH RATES

THE REFORM ACTS

REPEAL OF THE CORN LAWS

THE IRISH QUESTION

THE AMERICAN CIVIL WAR

THE CRIMEAN WAR

Alliances are dangerous things. I would not advise alliances with any nation but would cultivate friendship with all nations.

John Bright (1811-1889) was the second, and from the age of two the eldest, of the 12 children of a Rochdale cotton spinner. After schooldays he entered the family business but politics was in the blood. The abolition of the Test and Corporation Acts in 1828-9 enabled Friends (indeed, all dissenters) to stand in national and local elections. In 1833 Joseph Pease was the first Quaker to enter parliament. John Bright was the second, representing Manchester 1847-57 and Birmingham 1858-89. The six pennants show his main political preoccupations. From 1834 to 1841 he had been the leader of the anti-church party in his native Rochdale in a prolonged struggle about church rates. He first spoke against the corn laws in 1838 and was a founder member of the Anti-Corn Law League (1839), becoming its leading orator until the repeal of the laws in 1846. Anti-Corn Law china, *left*, asks 'Do you wish the food of your children to be taxed'. The statues are of, *right*, Richard Cobden (1804-1865), who drew Bright into the campaign, and Sir Robert Peel (1788-1850) who, when converted to repeal, piloted the bill through Parliament. On entering parliament Bright supported household suffrage in 1848, was a regular speaker in the debates between 1859 and 1867, and did not abandon the battle until 1884 when he believed the process completed – for he was, to the chagrin of his family, against women's suffrage. His courageous opposition to the Crimean war, *words at foot*, was on general policy rather than principle, for he was not an absolute pacifist: he gained the contempt of the prime minister, the respect of many MPs, and the distrust of his constituents. He was a firm supporter of Lincoln and the northern states in the American civil war. He carefully studied Irish issues from the time of the famine (*panel E8*), looking for land reform as a way forward but distrusting the nationalists and finally opposing Gladstone's Home Rule Bill of 1886.

Designed by Judi Grant; embroidered by Ann Castle and the Sidmouth group

The embroidered panel reads:

PUBLISHERS of TRUTH

The principal fountain of truth must be the Truth itself

Robert Barclay of Ury published his Apologia 1676

Others wrote
Journals + letters
Edward Burrough
Isaac Penington
Benjamin Clark
Mary Westwood
John Woolman
Job Scott.

Tracts were often printed by women and distributed by travelling ministers and packmen

B4 Publishers of Truth

'Friends of Truth' was one of the names Quakers used of themselves. God's Truth they saw as shown in the teaching of Jesus and the person of the inward Christ, a divine light in every human heart. The first publishers of Truth (*panel C1*) were those Friends who travelled at home and overseas, bearing witness to the universality of God's love and the need for inward experience to be shown in outward conduct. This panel commemorates the countless men and women who have published Truth by writing, printing and distributing books and pamphlets over the three and a half centuries of Quaker history (*for individuals see biographical notes*). 'Let all nations hear the word by sound or writing' wrote George Fox from Launceston gaol in 1656. 'Who hath writ more than the Quakers?' said 'our implacable adversary' Francis Bugg some 40 years later. Printing presses were authorised only in London, Oxford and Cambridge and books were required to be registered at Stationers Hall in London, the Star Chamber exercising censorship. Until 1695, when the

Licensing Act expired, Quaker publications could be issued only illegally and by printers prepared to take risks. Nevertheless, by 1700 some 4,000 items had emerged from the Quaker press, ranging from single sheets to 'collected works' of 500 pages or more. They were distributed to county quarterly meetings and area monthly meetings through a sort of compulsory book club – a practice not always relished by local Friends. A nineteenth century Orkney waggon, *bottom*, its bright cover made from re-used sailcloth from fishing boats, serves as a reminder that there were few places untouched, at one time or another, by the Quaker printed word.

Designed by Anne Wynn-Wilson; embroidered by Friends in Scotland

Stephen Grellet (1773-1855) belonged to an aristocratic French family. At 16, a refugee from the Revolution, he fled with his brother to Holland, South America and finally New York. Here, in 1795, he was convinced of Christianity and Quaker principles. In 1798 his gift in the vocal ministry was recognised. He paid four visits to Europe (1807-8, 1811-4, 1818-20, 1831-4), travelling extensively. One evening in late September 1807 he was at Quissac, near Congenies, in the south of France, where the villagers chose an orchard, *bottom*, for the meeting, 'placing lanterns in the trees, in which also many persons had taken their station': some 1,500 people were there. In 1818 he and William Allen (*panel E12*) while in Russia visited, *left*, Czar Alexander I, whom they had met in London in 1814. In 1819 he met, *right*, the aged Pope Pius VII - in front are a ragged woman, a Jewish rabbi, and a prisoner in chains – representing Grellet's concern for the whole of humanity. He is alone, *centre*, in front of a hut. The story is told of his feeling a call to visit a distant lumber camp only to find it abandoned. He sat in an empty hut and against all reason was impelled to rise and preach the gospel, which he did with much power. Years later he was accosted by a stranger in London who told him that he had been a lumberman and of evil life until, returning to a deserted camp for some forgotten tools, he heard a voice from within a hut and, as a result of listening, had lived a transformed life. While this story of 'preaching to nobody' has no firm grounding in history it symbolises Grellet's faithfulness to leadings. This faithfulness caused him, in 1813, on seeing the wretched conditions in the women's side of Newgate prison, to go to Elizabeth Fry, saying that something must be done, thus setting her on her life's work (*panel E5*).

Designed by Joe McCrum and Anne Wynn-Wilson; embroidered by the Leicester group

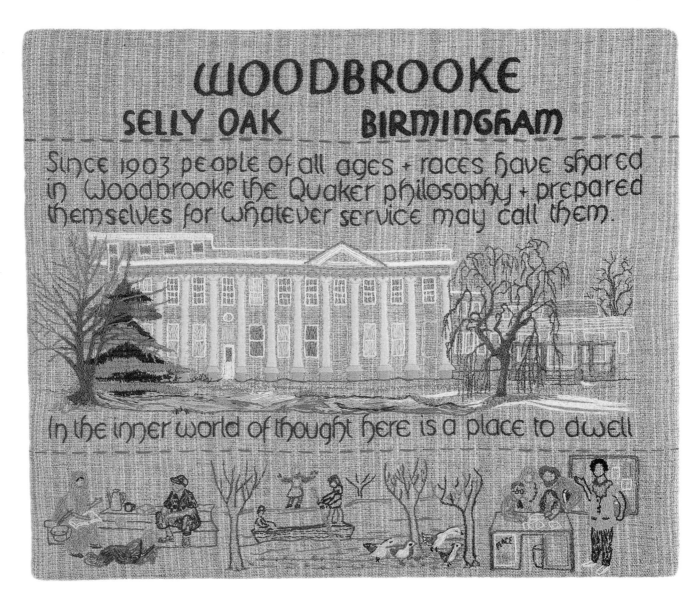

In the embroidered panel:

WOODBROOKE

SELLY OAK   BIRMINGHAM

Since 1903 people of all ages + races have shared in Woodbrooke the Quaker philosophy + prepared themselves for whatever service may call them.

In the inner world of thought here is a place to dwell

B6 **Woodbrooke**

As a direct result of the 1895 Manchester Conference (*panel A8*) some 700 British and Irish Quakers attended a summer school at Scarborough in 1897. World experts introduced sessions on Biblical history and criticism and the responsibilities of Christians in relation to social and international problems. Other smaller, more local, summer schools and settlements followed, and a growing awareness of need led John Wilhelm Rowntree to write 'A plea for a permanent settlement' – neither an academic theological college nor a narrow Bible school, though there would be emphasis on Bible study, in the expectation that there might be within the Society of Friends a deeper and more informed vocal ministry. The plea was answered through the gift by George Cadbury (1839-1922) of Woodbrooke, which had been his home between 1881 and 1894. Opened in 1903 it was the first of a federation of Selly Oak Colleges. The first director of studies, J. Rendel Harris (1852-1941), in accepting the post, had declined a chair at the University of Leyden. The resulting influx of Dutch students to Woodbrooke led to the first additional building being named Holland House. Rendel Harris was resolved that Woodbrooke should not only be international but that it should not be an introverted Quaker institution and that neither staff nor students should be restricted to members of the Society of Friends. The courses were adapted to changing needs and Woodbrooke also provided a home for students not engaged on its own courses. It has stressed flexibility of study whether for a year, a term, or a few weeks, and has always regarded extra-mural services as an integral part of its function. And the daily meeting for worship has been 'its core and the well-spring of all other activities'.

Design co-ordinated by Anne Wynn-Wilson from drawings by the Cotteridge group; embroidered by that group

SERVICE OVERSEAS

Be patterns, be examples in all countries — places — islands wherever you come that your carriage and life may preach among all sorts of people — George Fox

Quakers long held aloof from missionary work, lest it appear as a paid ministry. By the middle of the nineteenth century different views were prevailing and overseas work began in India in 1866 and in Madagascar the following year. In 1888 work began in Szechwan (Sichuan), west China. From Shanghai it was 1,000 miles up the Yangtze (Chang) to Ichang (Yichang), then 500 miles through the gorges, the boats pulled by trackers with bamboo ropes, *middle, lower left*. Out of educational work developed, outside the city of Chengtu (Chengdu), the West China Union University (1910), *middle, upper left*, later, the West China University of Medical Sciences. When, in 1897, slavery was abolished in Pemba, Friends started to run clove plantations, *right*, to help sustain the island's economy. First stage relief work often starts, *bottom, right of centre*, with emergency feeding. But self-sufficiency is achieved only by helping people to create a more fertile soil, whether it is the planting of trees or quite simple efforts to improve the garden produce of Ethiopian refugees in

Somalia, *centre*. A fertile soil depends on water. During the Indian famines of the 1890s George Swan (1869-1901), 'the boy from the fairground', helped the Gond villagers in mid-India to use simple materials to repair wells or dig new ones. In the 1950s a Canadian Quaker devised a method of concrete rings sunk to the required depth, *bottom right*. More is needed besides food and, *bottom left*, a Salvadorean refugee is being taught carpentering skills. Bread and skills are not enough: without personal relationships relief work can be arid. George Swan sat with the Gonds, laughing and talking with them and playing his concertina. In the same tradition, *bottom, left of centre*, a Quaker worker in the 1970s makes music with refugees in the Gaza strip.

Designed by Margery Levy; embroidered by several groups

B8 Quaker Peace Action Caravan

In May 1980 the Quaker Peace Action Caravan (the vision of Barry and Jill Wilsher) began its extensive travels, which continued until the end of 1985. In the course of those five and a half years it touched the imaginations – and the lives – of very many British and Irish Quakers and others, for it visited every monthly meeting area in the first 18 months. The group was concerned to stress individual responsibility for peace-making at the personal level, to examine political issues such as disarmament and human rights, and to strengthen the witness of Friends. It was in the tradition of Quakers who travelled in the ministry, like John Woolman and Stephen Grellet (*panels A6, B5*), who sustained the spiritual life of the Society and reached out with a message to others. In all, 20 people were involved in the caravan, two for the whole time, the rest for anything from a month to several years. By no means all were Friends, but all needed to be sympathetic to Quaker viewpoints. The team was dynamic and professional: 'Too many people in the peace movement accepted as unavoidable meetings that didn't start on time, inadequate resources and poor preparation; Q-PAC thought otherwise'. Violence it defined as 'anything which damages, degrades or destroys human beings' – and it explored the connections between the violence we do to each other in our everyday lives, violence in the community we live in, and the global violence which threatens the existence of the human race and our life on this planet. The team gave its message through street theatre, *left*, work in schools, *right* or simply in individual chance conversations, *bottom right*, stressing the worth of the individual and the conviction that, in the long run, individuals can change things.

Designed by Siw Wood and Frank Frisby; embroidered by Frank Frisby and the Minehead group

The embroidered panel depicts Swarthmoor Hall with the following text worked into the design:

SWARTHMOOR HALL
ULVERSTON in FURNESS

You may meet here if you will.
Judge Thomas Fell.
Margaret Fell.

Centre of comfort
administration and
inspiration.

1652-1702

A matter of sixty ministers did the
Lord raise up and send abroad out of the north country.

Swarthmoor Hall   C1

On Wednesday 16 June 1652 George Fox was at Preston Patrick (*panel B1*) and towards the end of the month he arrived at Swarthmoor Hall, near Ulverston. The visit was to prove of first importance for the next half-century of Quakerism. Swarthmoor was the home of Thomas and Margaret Fell and their (then) seven children, aged between two and 19. Thomas Fell, a circuit judge, was away from home when Fox arrived, returning to find his wife, children and servants 'bewitched by a travelling preacher' (as his alarmed neighbours told him). By now James Nayler (*panel A2*) and Richard Farnworth (d.1666) had arrived and the judge heard them and Fox sympathetically. Next day the newly-convinced Quakers were discussing where they should meet for worship and the judge, overhearing them, responded positively, *words top right* – no light gesture. Until the death of Margaret Fell in 1702 the Hall was of first importance as an administrative and pastoral centre for Friends. From 1654 onwards the 'first publishers of Truth' (*panel B4*) or 'valiant sixty' – mainly from

this part of England – travelled to the south of England, to the continent of Europe and to America with the Quaker message. The domestic, agricultural and industrial responsibilities of the Fell family, *centre and right*, necessitated a substantial household, a number of whom were among the valiant sixty, including Thomas Salthouse (1630-1691), who laboured chiefly in the south-west of England, and William Caton (1636-1665), who became the apostle of Quakerism in Holland. In 1759 Swarthmoor Hall ceased to be in possession of the Fell descendants. In 1912 it again became the home of members of the family and an option for its purchase by British Quakers, made possible with the generous help of American Friends, was informally fulfilled in 1952 and completed two years later.

Designed by Anne Wynn-Wilson; embroidered by Margaretta Playfair

C2 Margaret Fell

The driving energy, administrative flair and social position of Margaret Fell (1614-1702) profoundly affected the first fifty years of Quakerism. On ten occasions, the last when she was 84 years old, she travelled to London and back, *top left* – a journey of 500 miles. One of these was in June 1660 when, *centre*, she and Ann Curtis (1631?-1703) of Reading presented Charles II with a declaration on the peaceable nature of Friends' witness – Ann Curtis was the daughter of a former sheriff of Bristol, who in 1643 had been hanged for his loyalty to Charles I. Judge Fell had died in 1658. He never became a Quaker but would sit in his parlour (that is, study) at Swarthmoor with the door ajar while meeting for worship was being held in the great hall. After his death, neighbouring gentry sought to attack the Quaker movement. Fox was arrested and committed to prison at Lancaster in January 1664; next month Margaret Fell was imprisoned for having a meeting at her house. There they remained until the August assizes. She refused to promise to cease to have

meetings at her home so they tendered her the oath of allegiance which (*panel A9*) she conscientiously refused. The judge then pronounced the sentence of *praemunire*, placing her outside the king's protection and involving forfeiture of all her estate, real and personal, to the king, and life imprisonment. On hearing the sentence she made the response, *right*, and in the event her imprisonment, *top right*, came to an end in June 1668. She was imprisoned for a further year in 1670-1. Her seven daughters all became staunch Quakers but her son, George, was disaffected and attempted to wrest the Swarthmoor estate from his mother. When, in 1669, she married George Fox at Bristol, *bottom*, her seven daughters offered their support but her discontented son was absent.

Designed by Joe McCrum; embroidered by the Jordans group

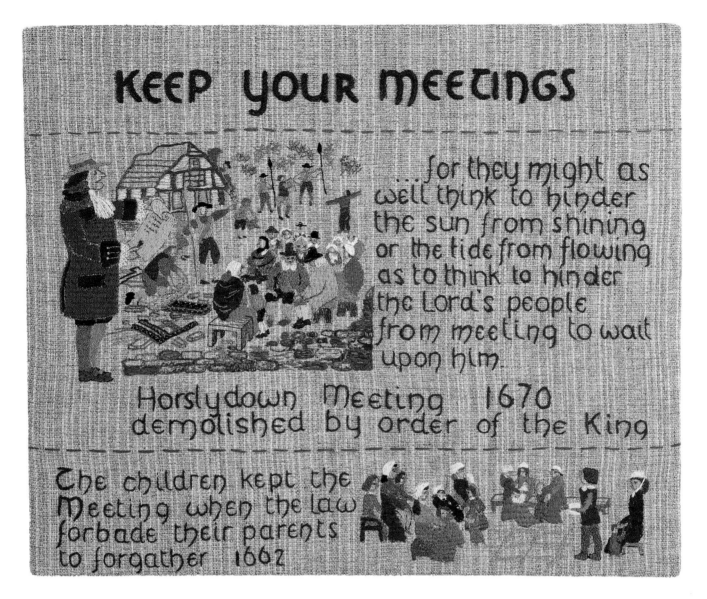

KEEP YOUR MEETINGS

...for they might as well think to hinder the sun from shining or the tide from flowing as to think to hinder the Lord's people from meeting to wait upon him.

Horslydown Meeting 1670 demolished by order of the King

The children kept the Meeting when the law forbade their parents to forgather 1662

It may be romantic to believe that early Friends met in secret, but it is not true. The presbyterian Richard Baxter (no friend to Quakers) wrote that 'many turned Quaker, because the Quakers kept their meetings openly and went to prison for it cheerfully [that is, bravely]'. The Quaker Act 1662 made it an offence for five or more of them to assemble 'at any one time, in any place, under the pretence of joining in a religious worship not authorised by the laws of this realm'. The Conventicle Act 1664 stiffened the penalties and extended the provisions to all nonconformists. In the spring and summer of 1664 nearly all the adult Friends in Reading were in prison for attending meeting and thus flouting the law. Not to be defeated, the children kept up the meeting, *bottom*, 'notwithstanding [the] wicked justice, when he came and found them there, with a staff that he had with a spear in it, would pull them out of the meeting and punch them in the back, till some of them have become black in the face'. On 29 July 1670, following the second Conventicle Act

(*panel F2*), the king in council, noting that Quakers met 'in Contempt of the Laws established' in their meeting house at Horsleydown, east of Southwark, ordered Christopher Wren (1632-1723), *left*, the king's surveyor, to 'cause the said House or Building to be pulled down, and demolished'. As a result 'a party of soldiers came with carpenters and pulled down the meeting-house and carried away the boards, windows, benches and forms, and sold them'. Friends met next day among the rubble, *centre*, until dragged off by soldiers, and it was six months before they were left in peace. Quakers had similar experiences elsewhere. The Toleration Act 1689 gave dissenters a degree of freedom of conscience, though many disabilities remained.

Designed and embroidered by the Reading group

The gathered meeting is the heart of the
MEETING HOUSE

Come with heart & mind prepared

C4 Meeting houses

Early Quakers met to worship wherever it was convenient, whether it was the great hall at Swarthmoor (*panel C1*) or in a farmhouse kitchen, or in the open air. But the need for 'a place of one's own' gradually led to the building of meeting houses or the adaptation of existing buildings. Up to the early nineteenth century Baptists, Independents (Congregationals), Presbyterians and Unitarians normally described their places of worship as meeting houses and it should not be assumed that a building so described had Quaker associations. The extreme simplicity of earlier meeting houses gave way to more elaborate buildings in the later eighteenth and nineteenth centuries. Those shown are, *upper row*, Manchester (1830), Jordans (1688), Hertford (1670), Broad Campden (1663), Burlington, New Jersey (1686) with, *behind it*, Blackheath (1972); and, *lower row*, Swarthmoor Hall, and then – with Friends House, London (1926) as a background – Come-to-Good, Cornwall (1709), Brigflatts (1675) and Drapers, Margate (c.1750). Four of the English

meeting houses were built before the Toleration Act 1689 – some 200 were in use before that date, two-thirds being purpose-built and often in conspicuous places in defiance of the authorities. While, out of the gathered silence, any of the worshippers might speak, it was early recognised that some had a particular gift in vocal ministry. These Friends, with the elders, sat on raised benches at one end of the room, the rest of the meeting facing them. The twentieth century saw the gradual discontinuance of the ministers' gallery or stand and the arrangement of benches, and later chairs, in a hollow square, *bottom*, or circle.

Designed by Anne Wynn-Wilson, meeting houses drawn by Maurice Green, worshippers by Joe McCrum; embroidered by Anne Wynn-Wilson, Ann Castle and several groups including Broad Campden

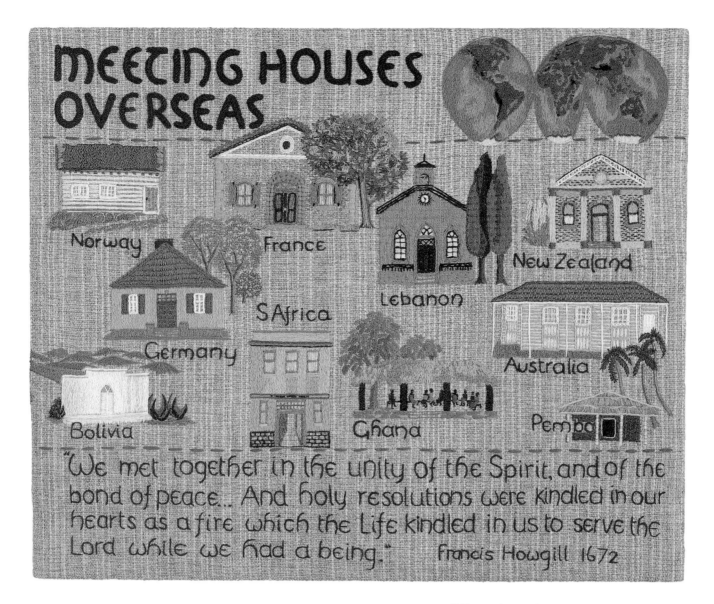

The ten meeting houses in this panel have different stories behind them. In the late eighteenth century groups of English ministering Friends travelling on the continent found small companies of likeminded people in the south of France and in Germany: meeting houses were built at Congénies (1822) and Pyrmont (1800, much rebuilt 1923). Similarly, James Backhouse (*panels D8, F20*) and Lindley Murray Hoag of New England found in 1853 a similar group at Botn in Röldal, Norway: a meeting house was built shortly afterwards. Missionary work by British and Irish Friends in the later nineteenth century led to the establishment of Brummana High School in the Lebanon, with its meeting house (1887), and to work among former slaves in Pemba after their liberation in 1897: the meeting house in Chake Chake (1959) was the third to be erected. Emigration of Friends to Australia and later to New Zealand and South Africa led to meeting houses such as Adelaide (1839, sent out from London in 69 packages), Auckland (1890, replaced by one on another site

1913) and Cape Town (1920, replaced by one on another site 1971). A number of Friends were associated with Achimota College in the Gold Coast (Ghana) and a wall-less meeting house was provided at Hill House (1934). No attempt has been made to depict the vast variety of meeting houses, sometimes called Friends' churches (*final panel*), on the North American continent. From the late nineteenth century Quakers in North America undertook considerable missionary work, particularly in East Africa, parts of Asia, and South America. Oregon Friends began work in Bolivia in 1930: the church at Jahuirkhatu is representative of the considerable missionary work of American Quakers as a whole.

Designed by David Butler; embroidered by several groups

C6 Meeting houses in the community

Though early meeting houses were used for schools (*panel C7*) and on occasion as an emergency refuge (*panel F6*) or in the nineteenth century for adult schools (*panel E7*), it was the twentieth century which saw a far wider use of them. Mosedale, Cumbria (1702), *top centre*, was closed as a meeting in 1865, though later re-opened for a few years. From 1936 to 1970 it was a chapel of ease for the Church of England. In 1973 it was reopened as a cafe for Lake District visitors and as a place of Quaker outreach. Brighton (1805), *top right*, started 'Fridays at Friends' in 1943 to provide informal hospitality to members of the forces: by 1948 this had developed into an adult education centre catering for 300 people. The central meeting house in Leeds was too large for Friends' needs and was replaced by a more modest one in 1987, *upper middle, left*, built so that it might be shared with Age Concern. Sidcot (1817), situated beside the school (*panel C7*), was remodelled in 1926, *middle, right*, so that it would be as much school hall as meeting house. When Winchester Friends

decided that they needed a meeting house they bought premises in 1974, *lower middle, left*, which would meet a variety of local needs as well as their own. At Wisbech (1854), *lower middle, centre*, part of the building was adapted in 1974 for sheltered housing for the elderly. The report *The Society of Friends and social service* (1944) envisaged 'a greater unity between the religious service of our meetings and the social service of Friends, since they are rooted in the same life and spirit'. Bury St Edmunds (1750), *bottom*, is one example of the ways premises have been used for some of the activities of the local community.

Designed by David Butler; embroidered by several groups in the meetings whose buildings are illustrated

Early schools were held in meetinghouses

As early as 1668 George Fox was urging setting up schools for boys and girls and many meetings did so, *bottom*, some being intermittent, others flourishing to outgrow the meeting house, as at Lancaster and Kendal. Most were held in the room women Friends used for their business meetings, where there was often a fireplace. In addition to these 'meeting schools' there were numerous 'private schools' conducted by individual Friends. Some of these eighteenth and nineteenth century private schools were small and restricted to Quaker children; others were widely known and patronised – like that at Ballitore, County Kildare, 1726-1836, where Edmund Burke (1729-1797) was educated; Newton-in-Bowland, Yorkshire, 1767-1911, where John Bright (*panel B3*) was a pupil; or Queenwood College, Hampshire, 1847-61, where the staff included scientists like John Tyndall (1820-1893) and Edward Frankland (1825-1899). During the later eighteenth century most 'meeting schools' declined and were replaced by larger 'committee schools' drawing on a

wider area for pupils: these were initially still small enough for the community to be known as 'the family'. *On the upper row* are The Mount, York (1857, formerly Castlegate, 1831); Lisburn, County Antrim (1774); Ackworth, near Pontefract (1779); Bootham, York (1846, formerly Lawrence Street, 1823) where the John Bright Library is depicted; and Sibford, near Banbury (1842). *Below* are Ayton, near Middlesbrough (1841, closed 1997); Saffron Walden, Essex (1879; originally Clerkenwell Workhouse, 1702; then Islington Road, 1786; then Croydon, 1825); Newtown, Waterford (1798); Leighton Park, Reading (1890) where the Peckover Hall is shown; and Sidcot, Somerset (1808).

Designed by David Butler and Avril & Ray Brown; embroidered by Ann Castle and the Bridport group

Seek to know one another in the things that **MARRIAGE** are eternal

Friends, I take this my friend to be my wife promising with God's help to be unto her a loving and faithful husband so long as we both shall live

CERTIFICATE OF MARRIAGE

Now these are to certify that for the solemnisation of their marriage this 28th day of Tenth Month, 1669 Thomas & Mary Ellwood appeared before a public meeting for worship

We sensibly felt the Lord with us and joining us, the sense whereof remained with us all our life
Thomas + Mary Ellwood 1669

C8 Marriage

In 1653 a commonwealth ordinance made compulsory a civil marriage ceremony before a justice of the peace. George Fox wrote: 'For the right joyning in marriage is the work of the Lord only, and not the priests or magistrates; for it is God's ordinance and not man's'. A Quaker marriage was therefore held as a meeting for worship in the course of which the couple made their declarations, which they confirmed by signing a certificate, later signed by all those present as witnesses. Though the precise wording of the declarations has changed over the years the essentials have been the same since the 1650s. After the Restoration in 1660 the church did not recognise Quaker marriages but they were upheld in the civil courts. Friends stressed the thoroughness of their preliminary enquiries, the fact that the meeting for worship was public, and their care to ensure efficient registration. Lord Hardwicke's Act 1753 implicitly recognised Quaker marriages in England & Wales and the Marriage Act 1836 did so explicitly. They were recognised in Ireland in 1844 and in Scotland in 1854. The law provided for the appointment by each area monthly meeting of a Friend as registering officer, *shown seated at table*, to ensure that procedure was in order. The couple shown in this panel are taken from the painting 'The Quaker wedding' by Percy Bigland (1856-1926), representing an early nineteenth century meeting. It is often said that Quakers disowned their members who 'married out'. In fact the disownment was for 'marriage before the priest', but it was not legally possible until the later nineteenth century for a Quaker to marry a non-Quaker in meeting. Changes in the law to permit this were secured in 1860 and 1872.

Designed by Joe McCrum; embroidered by Ann Castle and the Bournemouth & Swanage area monthly meeting group

QUAKER PILGRIMAGES

who knows on what far mountain of the spirit a vision awaits us

the Kingdom of Heaven did gather us and catch us all as in a net We came to know a place to stand in and what to wait in

In 1891 the young Ernest E. Taylor (1869-1955) moved from Malton, Yorkshire, to Kendal. He soon became captain of the mixed cycling club started by Westmorland Quakers when safety bicycles came in (*panel A8*). Not only were there carefully-planned Saturday expeditions but the chance to visit more distant Quaker meetings on Sundays. EET returned to Malton in 1905 with a lifelong interest in what he called 'the cradle of Quakerism'. In 1924 the tercentenary of George Fox's birth was commemorated by a five-day international conference in Kendal, attended by 400 Friends who, with Ernest Taylor as guide, visited the area round Sedbergh and Preston Patrick (*panel B1*) and Swarthmoor (*panels C1, C2*). In 1930 he followed this up with a 'pilgrimage' of mainly Yorkshire Friends. From 1936 there were regular expeditions to the north-west by senior pupils of Bootham and The Mount schools in York, and gradually all Quaker schools in England joined in. In the late 1940s Ernest Taylor found a successor in Elfrida Vipont Foulds (1902-1992). In 1952, following the third world conference of Friends, 650 Quakers from throughout the world spent a week in the north-west commemorating the tercentenary of the movement. After that, visits by individuals, meetings and other groups became a regular feature. Pilgrims are, *centre*, crossing the 'dangerous sands' of Morecambe Bay under the supervision of an official Duchy of Lancaster guide – this was the old route from Lancaster to the Furness district and thus to Swarthmoor. George Fox's vision on Pendle Hill of 'a great people to be gathered' is recalled, *top*, while, *bottom*, a group of pilgrims relaxes at the end of the day at the Old School, Yealand Conyers – Elfrida Vipont Foulds, *seated*, is recounting stories of the early Friends.

Designed and embroidered by Margaret Crosby and the north-west group

Children and young people

Until the twentieth century Quaker children sat in meetings for worship with their elders. Meetings normally lasted about two hours in the seventeenth and eighteenth centuries, an hour and a half in the nineteenth and about an hour in the twentieth. In Reading in 1664 (*panel C3*) the children kept up the meeting while their elders were in gaol; they also did this at Bristol and elsewhere. Not all Quaker children relished meeting – the Gurney girls (*panel E5*) found Norwich meeting tedious, one of them writing on 24 December 1797 that 'I spent *four* hours at Meeting! I never, never wish to see that nasty hole again'. Many other children, despite distracting thoughts during meeting, experienced a strong sense of belonging. By the 1920s there was a growing tendency to provide classes for children either before or after a short time in meeting. Friends in Britain in 1940 recorded their view that 'the Society of Friends may be compared to a family of which the young children are as much members as their parents and in which all, down to the youngest, can and may bear

their rightful share in the family life and interests'. The way in which this claim becomes a reality has varied from time to time and from meeting to meeting. The variety of provision for children, from care of toddlers, *centre left*, to teenage discussion, *centre right*, is drawn from the life in Colchester classes. Children have participated actively in the Quaker Tapestry through their drawings and also some of the embroidery – in 'The voyage of the *Woodhouse*' (*panel A5*) each child in the Nottingham group embroidered a different fish. In Britain, a junior yearly meeting began in the 1930s and developed as a conference for those between 16 and 18 – responsibility is as far as possible in the hands of the participants as a preparation for the entire self-government of those above 18 in the activities of Young Friends.

Designed and embroidered by the Colchester group

the LEAVENERS began as street theatre at Yearly Meeting Lancaster 1978

Leap

QFOC

to celebrate the creative spirit through the arts

In 1978, while the yearly meeting of Friends in Britain was in session at the University of Lancaster, there was great preparatory activity by the children and young people for a Quaker Festival. On Wednesday 16 August a 40-foot dragon was to be seen, *bottom*, in the Market Square. 'Up to the castle hill went the dragon, the children under its hessian spikes getting hotter and hotter and its great balloon eyes staring out over flaming jaws'. The dragon, symbol of aggression, was slain in front of the Castle; the newly-formed Leaveners mimed a parable about the triumph of love and peace over aggression; and in the rain, a Quaker meeting for worship was held. Next year the Leaveners – the Quaker Youth Theatre – produced *Quest of the golden age*, the first of a series of well-disciplined and exuberant performances, *centre*. The QYT went from strength to strength. One development was Theatre-Go-Round (1984), which worked with a group of young volunteers in Northern Ireland, both Protestant and Catholic. In 1988 exchange visits

began with Russian young people and in 1991 work in Romanian orphanages in association with the Concordia Theatre Company in Transylvania. In 1985 the Quaker Festival Orchestra & Chorus, *right*, was launched, bringing together young people and adults. Its opening performance at the Royal Festival Hall, Tony Biggin's choral drama *The gates of Greenham*, was packed out. The Leaveners Experimental Arts Project, *left*, was started because of a concern for youth unemployment, linking this with community arts (Leap Theatre Workshop, 1987) and the development of practical skills in conflict resolution (Leap Confronting Conflict, 1989).

Designed by Jack & Margaret Slade; embroidered by Cathy Spence and the Forest Hill group

George Fox: Lichfield, Pendle Hill

George Fox had been released from Derby gaol (*panel F1*) in early October 1651. Passing up the Trent valley, he 'espied three steeplehouse spires. They struck at my life and I asked Friends what they were, and they said, Lichfield'. Dictating his *Journal* 20 years later he had perhaps forgotten that the tallest spire was truncated, *left*, having been damaged in the civil war. A mile from the city Fox took off his shoes, leaving them with some shepherds, and walked through the city crying 'Woe unto the bloody city of Lichfield' – for 'there ran like a channel of blood down the streets and the market place was like a pool of blood'. He says that later he learned of the thousand Christians martyred during the time of the Emperor Diocletian, *the spires as his background*: yet more recent martyrs, *bottom left*, may have been deeply in his subconscious, for Joyce Lewis of Mancetter, close to his home, had been burned at Lichfield in 1557 during the Marian persecution, and Edward Wightman of Wyken, also nearby, had been burned there for heresy in 1612. After this incident at Lichfield, Fox travelled through the east midlands into Yorkshire: near Doncaster he met a small group of seekers with whom he had corresponded while in prison in Derby; near Wakefield he met with another. After some three months in east and north Yorkshire, he revisited the groups in the Doncaster and Wakefield areas about April 1652. With Richard Farnworth (d. 1666) he travelled north-west and 'spied a great high hill called Pendle Hill, *right*, and I went on the top of it with much ado, it was so steep . . . and the Lord let me see a-top of the hill in what places he had a great people to be gathered': with this vision in mind Fox continued north towards Sedbergh (*panel B1*).

Designed and embroidered by Anne Wynn-Wilson

QUAKER SIMPLICITY in all things both spiritual + material 1761

King George III asked to watch the Lord Mayor's Procession from the home of David Barclay

that the simplicity of truth may not wear out or be lost in our days nor in posterity, avoid pride and immodesty in apparel and all vain and superfluous fashions of the world. Yearly Meeting Epistle 1691

Quakers from the outset testified against 'vain superfluities' in dress and furniture, seeing these as expressions of pride. Thus Thomas Ellwood describes how he 'took off from my Apparel of those unnecessary Trimmings, of Lace Ribbands and useless Buttons, which had no real Service, but were set on only for what was, by Mistake, called Ornament'. But Quaker simplicity gradually ossified into Quaker uniformity, into a world of broad-brimmed hat and collarless coat, beaver hat or, later, bonnet, thee and thou, first day and sixth month. Margaret Fell in 1700 protested that 'we must look at no colours, nor make anything that is changeable colours as the hills are, nor sell them, nor wear them, but we must be all in one dress and one colour: this is a silly poor Gospel'. Yet it was 1860 before meetings ceased to be asked if Friends were faithful in 'plainness of speech, behaviour and apparel'. Many, in fact, were far from faithful. This panel depicts the scene in 1761 when George III asked David Barclay, an opulent London export merchant who lived in Cheapside, to be his host on the occasion of the Lord Mayor's procession. Barclay spared no expense in embellishing the house. Even if he did install panelling attributed to Grinling Gibbons he was firm on one point – the family should be dressed as plain Friends. His brother-in-law wryly remarked that 'on the whole they made a very genteel appearance, and acted their part in the masquerade very well'. The panel depicts the Queen and some of the Court in their splendour with, on either side, the Barclay family in their plainness.

Designed by Joe McCrum; embroidered by Ann Castle and the Bournemouth & Swanage area monthly meeting group

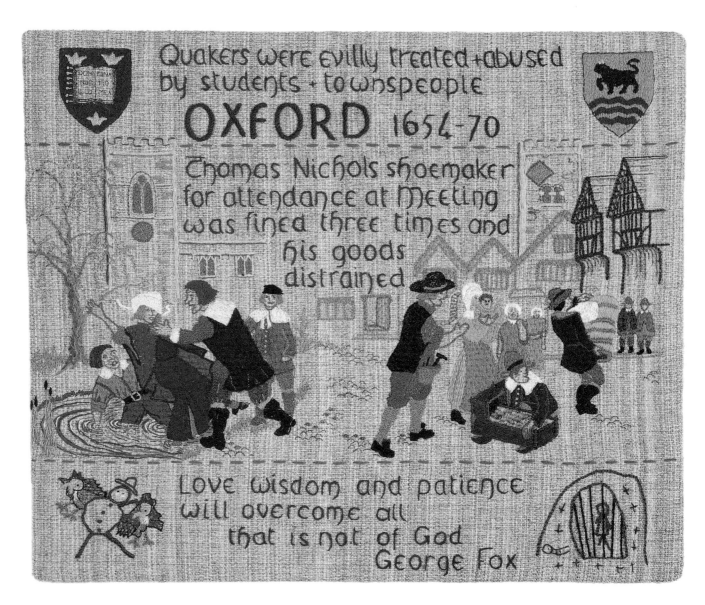

The image depicts an embroidered panel with the following text:

Quakers were evilly treated + abused by students + townspeople

OXFORD 1654-70

Thomas Nichols shoemaker for attendance at meeting was fined three times and his goods distrained

Love wisdom and patience will overcome all that is not of God
George Fox

D3 **Persecution in Oxford**

Though George Fox was gaining adherents in the east midlands in the late 1640s and in parts of Yorkshire in 1651, it was the 1652 Whitsun fortnight in the north-west that made of Quakerism a significant movement (*panels B1, C1*). It was from the north-west that most of the valiant sixty came: in late 1653 and 1654 they took the Quaker message to the south of England and overseas. The story of Oxford is typical of the opposition they received – and of the understanding sympathy. In 1654 Thomas Castle and Elizabeth Williams (who later caused a scandal and parted company with Friends) were harassed by both town and gown as they went about the city until at nightfall when they were, *left*, 'Hurry'ed into a Poole of watter called by the Name of Giles's Poole' – but the mayor, hearing of it, 'rescued them from that wick'd company, & conveyed them to the Mayor's house.' The mayor showed similar tolerance on later occasions and his son became a Quaker. Later that year a further seven men and five women came to Oxford from Kendal,

Yealand Redmayne, Preston Patrick and elsewhere, and a meeting was started at Richard Bettris's house, *right*. Persecution during the Commonwealth was sporadic: with the Restoration it became systematic and fiercer. Thomas Nichols (d. 1720), who lived opposite Jesus College, *right of centre*, was convicted and imprisoned many times for refusing to swear the oath of allegiance and for not attending church. In 1670, for attending meeting, all his goods and furniture were confiscated and he suffered further fines and imprisonments until the declaration of indulgence in 1686.

Designed by Anne Wynn-Wilson and Leslie Durham, incorporating drawings by Taunton children; embroidered by Margaret Ainger and the Oxford group

Coalbrookdale D4

In 1708 the Bristol brassfounder Abraham Darby I took over the leases of some furnaces in Coalbrookdale. The fuel problem for the industry was acute – even a century earlier the spoliation of woods by charcoal burners was a problem, and the seventeenth century saw several attempts to smelt iron with coal or coke instead of charcoal. By 1711 Darby found how to do this for his specialised business in cast-iron pots, kettles and other small ware. But it was not until mid-century that Abraham III was able to do away altogether with expensive charcoal-smelting: his breakthrough enabled the company to meet the growing demand from makers of nails and small ironware in the midlands. Throughout the eighteenth century the Coalbrookdale Company maintained its vigour, flexibility and pioneering spirit. While other industrialists were moving to country homes the Darbys lived in comfortable simplicity, close to 'the stupendous Bellows and mighty Cylinders' of the works and close to their workpeople. Their profits

were reinvested in the business, or devoted to the welfare of their workpeople, or used in philanthropy. On the other side of the Severn the non-Quaker ironmaster John Wilkinson had a growing business and in 1775 a group of subscribers met to consider the erection of a bridge, Abraham Darby III being foremost. It was cast at Coalbrookdale in 1778-9 and was formally opened on 1 January 1781. The panel shows, within the arch of the bridge, the industrial activities of the dale. The three Abrahams were active in Quaker affairs, both locally and further afield. Abraham II's wife Abiah (1719-1794) and Abraham III's sister-in-law Deborah (1754-1810) were well-known Friends who travelled in the ministry.

Designed by Joe McCrum; embroidered by the Bakewell and Sheffield groups

D5 Innocent trades

It was seventeenth century practice for shopkeepers to bargain, asking customers a higher price for their goods than they were prepared to take. George Fox wrote in 1656: 'Is it not better and more ease to have done at a word than ask double or more? This is deceitful before God and man'. Quaker shopkeepers, following this counsel, insisted on fixed prices. Customers who deserted them later found 'they might send any child and be as well used as themselves, so that all the inquiry was where there was a draper or shopkeeper or tailor or shoemaker that was a Quaker' – with the resultant cry of others that 'if we let these people alone they will take all the trading of the nation out of our hands'. Quaker testimony to simplicity meant that those going into trade could not in conscience manufacture superfluities; similarly, the testimony against all war meant that ironmasters could not manufacture cannon – trades had to be 'innocent'. Friends also counselled against covetousness and in this sense, too, trades had to be innocent. Stephen Crisp (1628 -

1692) of Colchester wrote in 1680: 'Take heed of enlarging your trades and traffics beyond your ability and beyond your capacity; for both these evils have been the ruin of some'. Most Friends avoided the temptation to stylish living and used their brains and money to put into practice new methods and new inventions. Hospitality at the time of the area monthly and regional quarterly meetings may also have been stimulating, for a farmer might find himself in the company of a pharmacist, an ironmaster, a wool-stapler and a grocer, and conversation could stimulate questioning and spark off new ideas. The panel shows, *bottom*, Luke Cock, a butcher, Daniel Quare, a clockmaker, and an anonymous grocer, representative of the daily work of a very substantial number of Friends.

Designed and embroidered by Irene Grey and the Newcastle (Northumberland) area monthly meeting group

Not slothful in business; fervent in spirit; serving the Lord.
QUAKER MERCHANTS
Romans XII.vii

Diligent in the management of their trades + affairs
Keeping their word + promises they gained credit in the country

Gervase Elam + sons
John Gurney
John Hustler
Newman Cash

Skipton
Blackburn Burnley
Bradford Leeds

Liverpool Leeds + Liverpool Canal 1770

The chief industry of the England in which Quakerism arose – the one regarded as the true 'staple' – was still wool. But the seventeenth century saw it becoming concentrated in a few areas, among them the north-west, the eastern counties, and Somerset. Considerable quantities of wool were spun into yarn round the Yorkshire-Westmorland border: this yarn fed not only the wool and 'shearman dyer' industries in Kendal but also in the West Riding of Yorkshire. Traditionally, clothiers distributed the yarn to handloom weavers working in their cottages, collecting the undyed cloth by packhorse, *right*, for finishing and for sale. But the seventeenth century saw also the beginnings of a move away from this system to a capitalist organisation of larger units – a move which was vastly accelerated by the introduction of machinery in the eighteenth century. The building of the impressive Leeds coloured (1758) and white (1775) cloth halls, *left and centre*, illustrates this change – similar halls were built elsewhere in the West

Riding. Some of the many Quaker wool-staplers are mentioned in the panel (*see biographical notes*). In the foreground two cloth merchants are displaying their wares and, *top*, is a factory, representing the change from the old domestic system. Distribution of completed goods was an increasing problem and it is not surprising that wool merchants and industrialists were foremost in the promotion of canals. As Hull was the nearest seaport accessible by water, merchants exporting to North America were anxious to use a west coast port and therefore were active from 1768 in promoting the Leeds & Liverpool Canal, which was begun in 1773 and completed in 1816.

Designed by Bette Dewhurst and Anne Wynn-Wilson; embroidered by Pat Butterfield and the Leeds area monthly meeting group

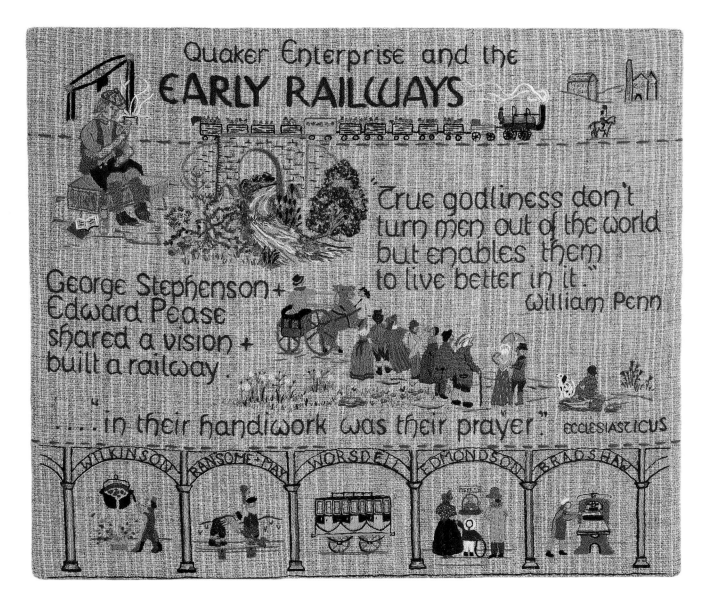

D7 **Railways**

As coal mining developed there were increasing problems getting the coal to the nearest river for shipment. From the early seventeenth century waggon ways began to be laid in Northumberland and County Durham, simple tracks of wooden planks on which small trucks could be pushed by boys or drawn by horses. These were developed at Coalbrookdale (*panel D4*), where wood gave way to cast iron. In 1818 Edward Pease of Darlington convened a meeting to promote such a waggon way from that town to Stockton. The Stockton & Darlington Railway Act received the royal assent on 19 April 1821. At the same time George Stephenson (1781-1848) and Nicholas Wood (1795-1865) met Edward Pease; the meeting was, despite romantic legend of their unheralded arrival, probably at Pease's request, and the two engineers had already traversed the proposed route. Stephenson had grown up in poverty and is shown, *top left*, sewing buttonholes to augment the slender finances of his youth. He was now the foremost engineer of the day

and in comfortable financial circumstances. Pease, though familiar with stationary steam engines, had not yet grasped the potential of steam locomotives, which Stephenson had first tried successfully in 1814: it was his persuasion that determined Pease to opt for them. The line was opened on 27 September 1825 and the panel recalls contemporary prints of the first train crossing Skerne Bridge, Darlington (as also depicted on the 1990 English £5 note). It was still conceived as a freight railway and passenger trains continued to be drawn by horses until 1833. Many other Quakers were involved in the development of railways and, *bottom*, are reminders (*see biographical notes*) of a few of them – and of one non-Quaker firm.

Designed and embroidered by the Leicester group

Quaker Botanists — Plant-hunters + Gardeners

Th Lawson · Jn Lettsom · Th Hanbury · Sy Parkinson · J Backhouse

Wm Curtis · Jn Bartram · Dn Oliver · Jn Fothergill · Pt Collinson · Jn Maddock

"...the universe is always singing and that man must learn to listen, so that his heart may join the universal chorus" 1887–1917 Sarah Martha Baker

Friends considered gardening and botany as innocent relaxations, likely to lead to habits of contemplation. They also gave attention to the remedial properties of plants and herbs. George Fox gave 25 acres in Philadelphia for a meeting house and school 'and to inclose another part for a garden, and to plant it with all sorts of physical plants for lads and lasses to learn simples there, and the uses to convert them to distilled waters, oils, ointments, etc.' (*panel D9*). This panel commemorates eleven Quakers who contributed to botany or the creation of gardens (*see biographical notes*) with a like number of plants with which they were associated – many were sent to Britain from North America by the indefatigible John Bartram. *Above* are *Magnolia grandiflora* (the great mountain variety, discovered by Bartram at Bull's Bay, South Carolina), *Phlox paniculata* (the pale purple variety, sent by Bartram, who called it *Lychnidea folio salicino*), *Collinsonia canadensis* (the horse balm Collinson introduced in 1735), *Lilium philadelphicum* (the bright orange lily

with a maroon lower half which, though taken home by French colonists in 1675, had been lost sight of till Bartram rediscovered it and, in 1737, sent bulbs to the Chelsea Physic Garden), *Dodecatheon meadia* (the so-called American cowslip, now claimed to have been introduced between 1617 and 1634 by John Tradescant the elder), *Hydrangea aborescens* (sent by Bartram in 1736). *Below* are *Chelone obliqua* (turtlehead, the late summer border plant, sent by Bartram), *Kalmia latifolia* (the olive-leafed mountain laurel, sent by Bartram), *Amaryllis curvifolia*, *Monarda didyma* (the scarlet bergamot collected by Bartram from Oswego, on the southern border of Lake Ontario, and sent in 1744), *Clematis florida* (imported from Japan by Fothergill about 1776).

Designed by Anne Wynn-Wilson; embroidered by the Quaker Tapestry embroidery teachers

In the image: True **HEALTH** springs from a balance of Body, Mind and Spirit.

Pharmacists

Jn. Fothergill 1712, Th. Hodgkin 80. 1795 1866 1827, Jos. Lister 1912

School Nurses

Apothecaries   overcrowding

Edinburgh University trained   antiseptics

Mental health William Tuke

Public Health — first Senior M.O.H.

General Practice Dr Alfred Salter 1875-1945 + Ada Salter

COMPASSIONE VOLONTANTE SERVIZENTE

Sir George Newman 1870 — 1945

a feeling heart is the first requisite of a surgeon *Joseph Lister*

SURGERY

BEALES BATHING MACHINE

The Retreat—York founded 1792

The Corner Shop Surgery Bermondsey

D9 True health

In the seventeenth and eighteenth centuries the apothecary was not only a practising dispenser and druggist but was also responsible for prescribing remedies, so that apprenticeship to him was a recognised entry into the medical profession, *top left*. Quakers, like other nonconformists, were barred until 1870 from entry to Oxford or Cambridge Universities so that those who wished to practise medicine were apprenticed to apothecaries, sometimes going on to Edinburgh University, then one of the foremost institutions – though Sarah Grubb (1756-1790) warned Friends against 'the pernicious principles instilled there'. Others went to Leyden and, from 1836, University College, London, was open to them. Quaker doctors have traditionally been concerned for preventive medicine. In the eighteenth century John Fothergill, *top, towards right*, increasingly put stress on diet and regular habits of life, including fresh air and exercise. In the twentieth century George Newman, *centre*, while medical officer of health for Finsbury, was concerned about

overcrowding, *top, towards left*, and himself went on inspections from midnight until 5 am, summer and winter, to find the actual number of men, women and children sleeping under incredibly horrible conditions. Similarly, the general practitioner Alfred Salter, *bottom right*, became an effective campaigner for better housing (*for these and others in the panel, see biographical notes*). William Tuke of York was largely responsible for promoting the establishment of The Retreat, *bottom left*, and thus pioneering a new approach to mental illness. More lightheartedly, Benjamin Beale's 1750 bathing machine, *bottom centre*, is a reminder of contemporary appreciation of the remedial effects of sea-bathing.

Designed by Margery Levy; embroidered by Margaretta Playfair and Friends throughout East Anglia

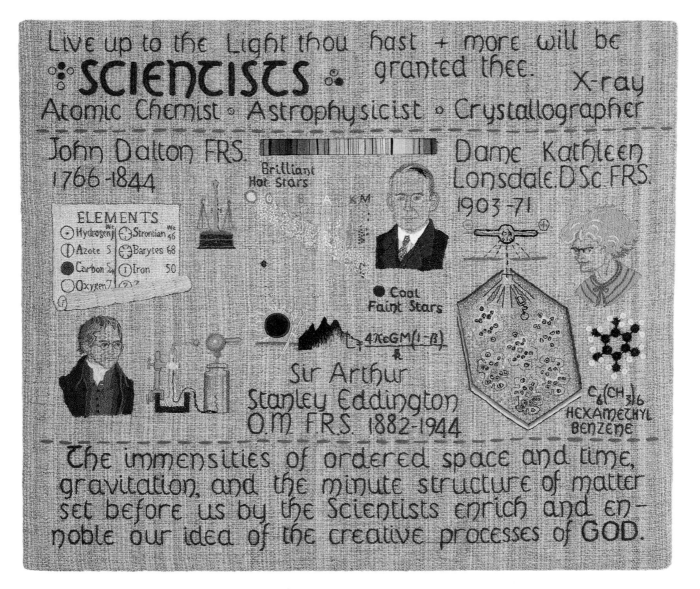

This panel commemorates three (*see biographical notes*) of some 80 Quakers who have (to 1997) been fellows of the Royal Society. The scroll, *left*, shows the symbols John Dalton used for some of the elements he worked with and the atomic weights he derived. The apparatus, *right of his portrait*, is a chemical balance and glass tube inverted in a reservoir of mercury – the tube is furnished with electrical contacts and connected to an electrostatic generator to cause a spark in an explosive mixture of gases. He used this to determine the simple proportions in which elements combined. Arthur Eddington's work in astronomy is represented by the sun's spectrum, *middle top*, and the diagram, which shows the life cycle of stars – progressing from young stars, reddish in colour, dim and relatively cool, to older stars, brighter, hotter, larger and bluer as they age, *lower right to top left, below the spectrum*. During an eclipse of the sun, Eddington was able to photograph a star behind the sun, thus confirming Einstein's theory. The sun, *centre*, is

shown eclipsed over the volcanic profile of the Isle of Principe. The equation, *centre*, relates the deviation of the light to the mass of the sun. Kathleen Lonsdale's early experiments were with a crystal, *below her portrait*, of hexamethyl benzene which consisted of six groups of carbon and hydrogen atoms linked together. A diagramatic representation of an X-ray tube, *right*, has a screen with a hole in it, allowing a narrow beam of X-ray to impinge on a crystal. The beam is scattered by the regular structure of the crystal and produces characteristic patterns on a photographic plate, from which Kathleen Lonsdale learned to deduce the precise structure of the crystal.

Designed and embroidered by Winifred Booker and the Liskeard & Looe group

Since the 17. INDUSTRIAL WELFARE has developed as an expression of Quaker faith

CHEAPER CORN SHIPPED • ORE STOCKPILED • 1704 LONDON LEAD CO • "The Gospel must be Social" JOHN WILHELM ROWNTREE • TOWN PLANNING NEW EARSWICK 1903 • ROWNTREE • BREAKFAST ROOM WORKING CLOTHES • PROVISION FOR OLD AGE 1895 BOURNVILLE GARDENS • HUNTLEY & PALMER 1849 • CADBURY • HEALTH • EDUCATION • SPORT

D11   Industrial welfare

This panel commemorates four Quaker firms who have pioneered industrial welfare. From the early eighteenth century the London Lead Company, with interests in Northumberland, Derbyshire, and north Wales, promoted imaginative schemes including, at a time of prohibitive retail food prices, purchase of bulk foods wholesale, sold to their employees at cost price, *top left*. In 1879 Richard Cadbury (1835-1899) and his brother George (1839-1922) daringly moved their factory from central Birmingham to Bournville, created a garden village with houses at affordable rents, and encouraged tenants to cultivate vegetables and fruit in their gardens, *centre right*; they later added almshouses for the elderly, *centre*. In 1904 Joseph Rowntree, who likewise had moved his factory from central York, planned New Earswick on similar lines. Huntley & Palmers provided a room for their workers to take breakfast, *centre left*. Provision by various firms of nursing care, part-time further education, and sports facilities, *bottom*, may now seem paternalistic – and it must be acknowledged that Huntley & Palmers' nineteenth century wages were not above reproach. Nevertheless, these pioneering schemes met the needs of the times. Before 1909, when Britain introduced old age pensions, ageing employees could pose a moral dilemma. Though Joseph Rowntree sometimes helped longstanding employees personally if they needed help in retirement, he knew that this was an outdated approach and in the 1890s began to think about a pension scheme, just as his father had thought about an insurance scheme (*panel E11*). It would be expensive to start and complex to administer but he knew this was the way forward and when, in 1906, it was finally set up the 4,000 employees were in an assured position against retirement.

Designed by Margery Levy; embroidered by Hilda Jenks and the Selly Oak group

Cherish the beauty + variety of his world

QUERY 19

Are you concerned that man's increasing power over nature should not be used irresponsibly but with reverence for life and with a sense of the splendour of God's continuing creation?

British Quakers (like those in many other places) have long maintained and regularly revised a collection of *Advices and queries* designed to foster spiritual alertness and an awareness of the practical implications of religious conviction. The 1964 revision contained for the first time reference to responsibility for the environment, *top and bottom*. In 1994 *Advices and queries* were again revised and include the words: 'We do not own the world, and its riches are not ours to dispose of at will'. This panel questions our stewardship. Pollution – smoke and noxious gases from industry and transport – is depicted, *top*, while alternatives based on energy-saving principles are shown *centre*. Children embroidered the 'free-range' ducks emerging from the lake – and the frog in the undergrowth represents one endangered species. In a farm worked by organic husbandry, *top left*, hedges guard against soil erosion and companion plantings (such as onions and carrots with marigolds and aromatic herbs) deter pests. Over the years Quakers have

taken often small steps towards a more responsible use of the earth's resources. Thus John William Graham (1859-1932) of Manchester campaigned vigorously against the pollution of smoke and was at one time chairman of the Smoke Abatement League. F. Newman Turner (1913-1964) developed ideas of organic farming and practised them from 1939. He founded and edited *The farmer* to advocate these and natural health for animals at a time when more orthodox journals were reluctant to accept articles of so revolutionary a kind. He believed that real health was possible only if food is grown naturally in a healthy environment – and thus that ecology and true health are inseparably linked.

Designed by Anne Wynn-Wilson; embroidered by Ann Nichols and the Wokingham group

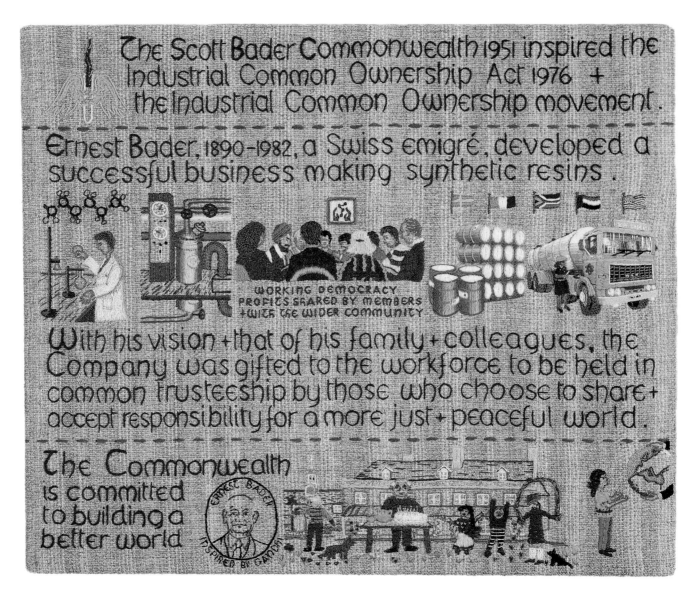

The Scott Bader Commonwealth 1951 inspired the
Industrial Common Ownership Act 1976 +
the Industrial Common Ownership movement.

Ernest Bader, 1890-1982, a Swiss emigré, developed a
successful business making synthetic resins.

WORKING DEMOCRACY
PROFITS SHARED BY MEMBERS
+WITH THE WIDER COMMUNITY

With his vision + that of his family + colleagues, the
Company was gifted to the workforce to be held in
common trusteeship by those who choose to share +
accept responsibility for a more just + peaceful world.

The Commonwealth
is committed
to building a
better world

ERNEST BADER
INSPIRED BY GANDHI

D 13   Scott Bader Commonwealth

In 1912 Ernest Bader (1890-1982), *bottom left*, came
to England from Switzerland and in 1923 founded
Scott Bader & Company, to sell Swiss celluloid. The
company then acquired an agency for nitro-cellulose
and other products which advanced the swifter
application and durability of paints and lacquers. In
1932 the company started manufacturing pigment
pastes for surface coatings and in 1940, disrupted by
air raids, left London for a Georgian manor house,
bottom, in 44 acres of park in Wollaston, near
Wellingborough, Northamptonshire. Here, it
pioneered the manufacture of synthetic resins,
introducing the first styrenated polyester resin,
middle left, outside the United States. As a result, the
company played a leading role in founding the glass
reinforced plastics industry, notably in boat
building. Ernest Bader and his wife, Dora Scott,
joined the Society of Friends in 1945. He was an
industrial realist but also an idealist. After serving in
the Swiss army, he became a pacifist in 1915. In 1951,
in order to achieve workforce participation and

responsibility and to create industrial democracy, he
and the other shareholders gave their shares to the
newly-formed Scott Bader Commonwealth, *centre*.
The commonwealth, a company limited by
guarantee and a registered charity, holds the Scott
Bader Company in trust. Membership of the
commonwealth is open to those employees who
believe in the principles and accept the
responsibilities of common trusteeship – a
fundamental change of concept described by Ernest
F. Schumacher in *Small is beautiful* (1973): 'it would
be better to think of such a transfer as effecting the
extinction of private ownership rather than the
establishment of collective ownership'.

*Designed by Anne Wynn-Wilson, Ann Nichols, Hansi
Bader and commonwealth members; embroidered by
Vivienne Schilt, Joan Swift and others in Northampton &
Wellingborough area monthly meeting*

In the embroidered panel:

GEORGE FOX at ULVERSTON
his experience of true healing

"I looked at it in the love of God...
and the Lords power sprang through me and
through my hand." G.F. Journal

George Fox at Ulverston: healing   E1

This panel depicts a scene in late 1652. After Fox's first visit to Swarthmoor (*panel C1*) he had been in Kendal, Lancaster and the neighbourhood before returning towards autumn. On a lecture day in Ulverston parish church (an innovation of the presbyterians) Priest Lampit (1605?-1677) was 'blustering on in his preaching' and, after an interchange between him, Justice Sawrey and Fox, 'all the people in the steeplehouse were in an outrage and an uproar', dragging Fox from the church and town through mire and dirt to the common moss. There he was beaten with willow rods, hedge stakes, clubs and staves, a mason finally giving his hand a blow with his rule staff so that the skin was struck off and the blood came. Then the people cried out, 'He hath spoiled his hand for ever having any use of it more'. Fox, 'in the love of God to them all that had persecuted me', then had the experience recounted, *bottom*. Nevertheless, he added that 'my body and arms were yellow, black and blue with the blows and bruises that I received amongst them that day'.

Seven years later, when he was in London, Sarah Blackberry (d.1665) came to tell him how many poor Friends were in want. That afternoon, with his encouragement, she convened a meeting of 60 women Friends who would be able, in visiting the sick 'in the Lord's Power and Word, by the same Power to heal and strengthen with the outward things and without them'. The long-lost 'Book of miracles' performed by Fox is best understood as a series of healings by naturalistic medical cures and, perhaps as much, by his empathetic gifts and encouragement. Inward and outward were seen as inseparable and one was not to be set against the other.

Designed and embroidered by Anne Wynn-Wilson, Wendy Gillett and others

'a very phenomenon in the history of political economy' ~ Karl Marx

JOHN BELLERS 1654 ~ 1725

To the Lords + Commons in Parliament Assembled

proposals
1695 a colledge of industry
1697 education of children
1699, 1714 and 1723 protection of poor and no death penalty for fellons
1710 an European State and Council of Christian persuasion
1712 ease of elections
1714 improvement of physick

1702 1714 Queen Anne

the poor without imployment are as rough diamonds

their worth is unknown

E2 John Bellers

Manual workers fared badly in the second half of the seventeenth century, for wages did not keep pace with the rising price of necessities and much social legislation was repressive in effect if not in intention. London Quakers in the 1670s set up a fund to buy flax to be given to poor Friends to spin, afterwards sending it to be woven into cloth, and in 1680 John Bellers took over the financial management from William Meade (*panel F2*). Bellers saw that immediate relief was not enough and sought to grapple with the causes of poverty. His mind ranged widely over social and international issues on which he wrote, *top left*, prolifically and succinctly: some of the 20 titles, *left*, were addressed to parliament or to Queen Anne, *right*. In a preface to *Essays about the poor* (1699) he dryly commented: 'Some may think me too short in expression. I desire such, if they are at leisure, to read this tract twice; and it will then be more intelligible to them'. In one tract he commended giving baked beef to prisoners and towards the end of his life, *bottom left*, 'treated 58 of my Poorer neighbours with the

same fare to their Sattisfaction & but about 3d head cost'. On the poor, *bottom, left of centre*, he wrote: 'Its as much more Charity to put the Poor in a way to live by honest Labour, than to maintain them Idle, as it would be to set a mans broken leg, that he might go himself, rather than always to carry him'. On education, *bottom, right of centre*: 'The Children called The Black-Guard are our Neighbours, our Flesh and Blood, however mean and contemptible they now appear. How much is owing to Birth and Education, that hath made the Difference between them and us?'. And on the abolition of the death penalty for everything but murder, *bottom right*, 'How sincerely can we say the Lord's Prayer *Forgive us our Trespasses*; when for the loss, possibly, of less than 20 Shillings, we Prosecute a Man to Death?'.

Designed and embroidered by Daphne Boothby and the Hammersmith group

The Quaker Trade of
BANKERING
Many Quaker Banks merged to form the core of well known Companies

Jonathan Backhouse balances the cash 1819

Honesty in business and the payment in full of debts justly incurred

JONATHAN BACKHOUSE & CO

Bankering E3

In the seventeenth century London goldsmiths became recognisable as bankers, but with the formation of the Bank of England (1694) their own banknotes fell into disuse. Among these goldsmith bankers was the Quaker John Freame (1665-1745), whose son in 1736 took as partner James Barclay (1708-1766). Save for 1766-76 the name Barclay has been included in the title ever since. There were very few private provincial banks until the mid-eighteenth century but development was then rapid – some 150 in 1776, 350 in 1800 and 430 in 1833 (most issuing their own notes). Many Quakers were among them – Sampson Lloyd II (1699-1779), the Birmingham ironmaster, was founding partner of Taylor & Lloyds (1765); the Norwich woolstaplers opened the bank John & Henry Gurney & Co. (1775); and there were a multitude of smaller banks. This panel is about an incident in the history of the Backhouse Bank (1774) in Darlington. Jonathan Backhouse had been active in promoting a railway from the town to Stockton (*panel D7*) and the

proposed route would have destroyed the fox coverts of Lord Darlington (1766-1842), a noted hunter and patron of the turf. He determined in revenge to break the bank and ordered his tenants to pay their rent in Backhouse notes, intending to present them and demand more gold than the bank could cover. Backhouse, getting wind of this, hastened to London to replenish his ready gold but on the return journey the coach lost a forewheel at Croft Bridge, just short of the town. 'Balancing the cash' by piling it on the opposite side of the coach, he delivered the gold to the bank in time to honour the large parcel of notes presented by Lord Darlington's agent. The bank's accounts for 25 June 1819 record 'To Bank and Cash to London £32,000' and there is a later debit entry of £2.3.0 for a wheel.

Designed by Joe McCrum and the Darlington group; embroidered by that group

As a Quaker I believe there is that of God in all people, though it's sometimes hard to find. Punishment ought to be a way of helping people to realise the hurt they are doing to this sense of worth in themselves + in others.
Harvey Gillman

E4 **Criminal justice**

Very many early Friends had experience of the appalling conditions in seventeenth century gaols (*panels A3, F1, C2, etc.*) and, *bottom left*, George Fox is depicted in Scarborough Castle, where 'the wind drove in the rain forcibly, so that the water came over my bed and ran about the room, that I was fain to skim it up with a platter'. Many eighteenth century ministering Friends visited prisons; the work of Elizabeth Fry (*panels E5, E6*) and others brought penal conditions into greater prominence; British Friends from 1818 onwards urged the complete abolition of the death penalty; William Tallack (1831-1908), a London Friend, was secretary of the Society for the Abolition of Capital Punishment from 1863 to 1866, when he became secretary of the newly-formed Howard Association for the Prevention of Crime, a post he filled for 35 years, concerned not only to improve prison conditions but to tackle poor housing and unemployment which he saw as roots of much crime. The imprisonment of large numbers of

Friends as conscientious objectors during the first world war (*panel A7*) provided personal experience of penal conditions which proved invaluable in the development of Quaker concern. Many Quakers have been justices and Geraldine Cadbury (1865-1941) pioneered the creation of children's courts with a more relaxed atmosphere. Some Friends have entered the prison service; others have worked in the probation service, in approved schools, or have pioneered communities in which disturbed children and adolescents can work through their difficulties. Yet others have questioned the whole penal system. A young man is shown, *bottom*, doing community service; a family visiting a prisoner; and a prison officer carrying keys.

Designed by Ann Castle; embroidered by the Mid-Somerset area monthly meeting group

By her inspiration devotion + charm she attracted public support for her concern to lighten the suffering + humiliation of prisoners

ELIZABETH FRY 1780 1845
Lord·I believe·help thou my unbelief

Elizabeth Fry (1780-1845) was the fourth of the 11 children of John Gurney (1749-1809), 'handsome Johnny', a wealthy Norwich wool-stapler. From 1786 the family lived in style at Earlham Hall, two miles outside the city: plain Friends looked askance at their worldliness, fashionable dress and sumptuous dances. The children were lively and are shown, *bottom*, holding up the London mail as it approached Norwich. A profound religious experience at 18 led Betsy (as she was known) to give up this carefree life – to her sisters' distress. In 1800 she married Joseph Fry (1777-1861), a London merchant, and in 1813 Stephen Grellet (*panel B5*) told her of the desperate conditions in the women's side of Newgate prison. She immediately sent out for flannel, gathered a group of young women Friends and next day visited the prison with garments for the babies. She appealed to the mothers' basic human dignity and persuaded them, *left*, to co-operate in turning chaos into order: they listened, intent, while she read from the Bible. In 1817 she set up the Association for the

Improvement of the Female Prisoners in Newgate (popularly, the Ladies Association): a school was established, a matron appointed, and the following year a House of Commons committee, *right*, congratulated her on her achievements. In 1832, however, the mood had changed and she was closely questioned as to 'whether her views did not tend to the encouragement of crime rather than its prevention' – for by then the treadmill was seen by the authorities as preferable to needlework. She was not only a prison reformer, however – the Bible Society and anti-slavery movement had her active support. She was an indefatigible correspondent and traveller: her frequent journeys in the British Isles and on the continent combined Quaker religious service with her many other interests.

Designed by Joe McCrum; embroidered by Hilda Jenks and the Selly Oak group

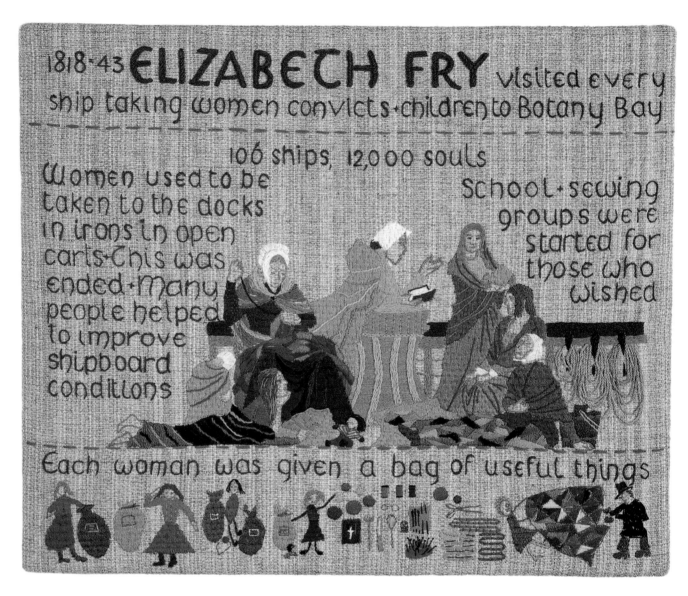

The embroidered panel reads:

1818-43 **ELIZABETH FRY** visited every ship taking women convicts·children to Botany Bay

106 ships, 12,000 souls

Women used to be taken to the docks in irons in open carts·This was ended·Many people helped to improve shipboard conditions

School·sewing groups were started for those who wished

Each woman was given a bag of useful things

E6 **Elizabeth Fry and the patchwork quilts**

Newgate was a centre where women prisoners from all over the country were collected before transportation to Australia. They were accustomed to riot on the eve of departure – for next day they would be clapped in irons and driven to the waterside in open waggons amid jeering crowds. In the summer of 1818 Elizabeth Fry (1780-1845) went to the governor and promised to accompany them if they were sent in closed hackney carriages. He consented and she proved her point for there was no riot and their departure was orderly. There were 128 convicts and many bewildered children. She divided them into classes of 12, each electing a monitor. With the help of her Ladies Association it was arranged that each woman would receive gifts, including one Bible, two aprons, one black cotton cap, one large hessian bag to keep her clothes in, and one small bag containing a piece of tape, an ounce of pins, 100 needles, nine balls of sewing cotton in different colours, 24 hanks of coloured thread, eight darning needles and one small bodkin. In addition

there were two stay laces, a thimble, a pair of scissors, a pair of spectacles if needed, two pounds of patchwork pieces, two combs, a knife and fork and a ball of string. There was all the equipment to make a patchwork quilt. The work of quilting would be an occupation during the tedious journey to Australia, and the quilt might be sold for a guinea at Rio de Janeiro or on arrival in Australia. It would also be a testimonial to her skills as a needlewoman thus giving her a hope of proper employment instead of being forced into prostitution. Elizabeth Fry and another Quaker visited, with one exception, every convict ship until 1841.

Designed by Joe McCrum and Anne Wynn-Wilson; embroidered by Ann Castle and Friends in Australia; bottom section drawn by Taunton children and embroidered by them and children in Australia

FIRST DAY SCHOOLS and the
ADULT SCHOOLS MOVEMENT
—the ideas of religion · service ·
education and fellowship
were held together

1847–1904
Forty Thousand
Birmingham
Early morning students
joined classes in the
Institutes

Pioneers of the movement
Joseph Sturge
Samuel Fox
William White
Joseph Rowntree

Love not dogma, life
not creeds

The beginning of the adult school movement is usually credited to William Singleton, a member of the Methodist New Connexion, who opened a school in Nottingham in 1798. He was helped at an early stage by the young Quaker grocer Samuel Fox (1781-1868), whose premises were used and who early developed a school for working women. Evangelicals in all denominations, finding that so many men and women were unable to read the Bible, gave impetus to the movement. The Friends First Day School Association (1847) was founded by some of the pioneers (*see biographical notes*) to provide a forum for discussion among adult school teachers. The next half-century saw rapid growth. In 1901 there were 30,060 registered scholars with an average weekly attendance of 18,183: since 1896, however, there had been a steady decline in the men's schools though this was more than compensated by the increase in the women's. To broaden the basis an interdenominational National Council of Adult School Associations (1899;

National Adult School Union, 1914) was formed in place of the Quaker organisation but a variety of social and educational factors led to a severe decline in membership in the inter-war years. The great days of the later nineteenth century are described by Charles Booth (1840-1916), author of the 17-volume *Life and labour of the people of London* (1891-1903) and no ready enthusiast, as providing 'a very strong religious diet for those who find what they need not in sitting under some gifted teacher but in open, equal, individualistic democratic debate on the meaning of the Word of God and the interchange of spiritual experience, their leader being no more than the chairman of their meeting'.

Designed by Anne Wynn-Wilson; embroidered by the Northampton & Wellingborough area monthly meeting group

The GREAT HUNGER

Potato Famine in Ireland

1845-48

1,500,000 died of starvation & 1,000,000 emigrated-
Irish Friends were entrusted with international relief
funds to feed the starving, replenish seed & to redeem
fishing nets & tools which had been pawned for food.

E8 Ireland: The great hunger 1845-8

The 1841 census showed that, of Ireland's eight million population, nearly three and a half million occupied 'the lowest class of house accommodation', the potato being almost their only food as well as their chief means of getting the other necessities of life. There had been failures of the potato crop in 1822, 1831-2 and 1845, but none on the scale of 1846 when not only did the potato fail on an unprecedented scale but wheat, barley and oats were all of them poor. Various relief organisations were set up during the autumn and on 13 November Irish Quakers formed a Central Relief Committee in Dublin with four auxiliary committees to take responsibility for the worst-hit areas. At the same time a committee of 20 British Friends was appointed and William Forster (1784-1854) of Norwich visited, under the guidance of the Dublin committee, the stricken areas of the west. He saw children 'worn to skeletons, their limbs wasted almost to the bone' and a widow with two children who had lived the whole of the week on two quarts of meal and two heads of cabbage. Pigs and poultry had disappeared because the poor could no longer feed them – though this destitution was side by side with plenty for the more affluent elsewhere. Soup kitchens were established and clothing distributions undertaken. Over 36,000 lbs of seeds were distributed to 40,000 people so that nearly 10,000 acres were sown, and fisheries were promoted. Not all efforts were equally successful but by the time the committee had finished its work in 1852 it had handled the considerable sum of £100,000 – this included the value of much food received from America and, nearer home, 56 boilers given by the Coalbrookdale Company (*panel D4*).

Designed and embroidered by the Wigham family and the Dublin & Waterford groups

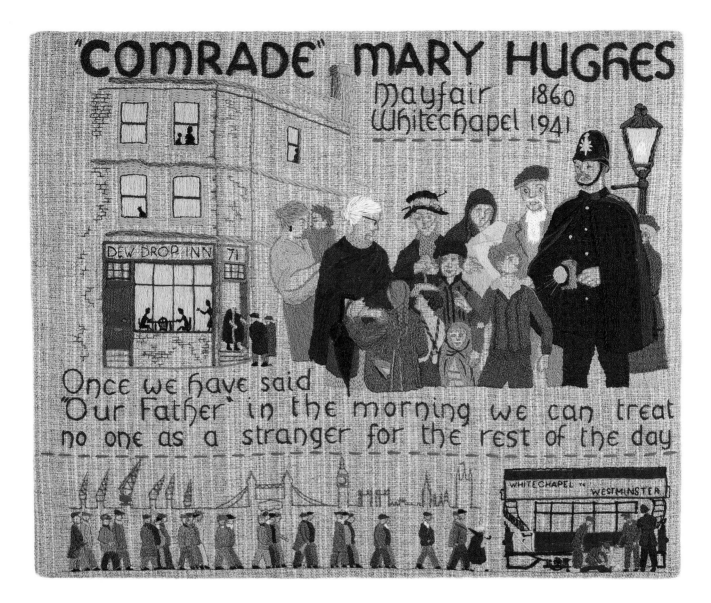

Mary Hughes E9

Mary Hughes (1860-1941) is shown, *centre*, in the red cloak she habitually wore in later life. She was the daughter of Thomas Hughes (1822-1896), a county court judge, author of *Tom Brown's schooldays* (1857), and a leading Christian socialist with F. D. Maurice (1805-1872) and Charles Kingsley (1819-1875). She saw the needs of the working poor in rural Berkshire, but when she came to London in the 1890s and saw the poverty in Whitechapel she determined to live there and devote herself to her neighbours. She had been occasionally to Friends' meetings at Hitchin and Falmouth in the 1870s but it was the attitude of the Church of England to the first world war that made her decide to throw in her lot with Quakers – she joined the Society in 1918. She was a member of the Stepney Board of Guardians (the first woman – and she fought to get the inmates tea), a Labour councillor (she never canvassed) and a justice of the peace, but it was her unconventional and instinctive response to people that made her beloved. In 1926 she bought a disused public house in Vallance Road, Whitechapel, renaming it, *left*. She spent little time or energy on herself – her staple diet was tea, margarine, onions, bread, cabbage and milkless cocoa. The door was always open to callers and this small, wiry, energetic woman was always first on the scene in distress or emergency. In her seventies she was leading a march of the unemployed from the East End to the Houses of Parliament, *bottom*, when she was knocked down by a tram. Disregarding the ambulance, she summoned the young tram driver and made him write: 'I am entirely responsible for this accident. The tram driver is in no way to blame'. Then, signing it 'Mary Hughes JP', she said, 'Now you can do what you like with me'.

Designed by Joe McCrum and Anne Wynn-Wilson; embroidered by the Westminster group

E10 Unemployment

The year 1926 was a critical one in South Wales. At the end of a prolonged national coal strike (including a nine-day general strike) the miners were left with a cut in wages, a longer working day and on occasion victimisation. And some pits did not reopen. Following the yearly meeting of British Quakers in late May, Emma Noble (1886-1956), the wife of a Swindon railwayman, felt impelled to go and find out for herself what things were like. A Quaker doctor advised her to go to the Rhondda, some fifteen miles north of Cardiff: she spent a week talking to local councillors, officials, teachers and poor law guardians and, back at home, appealed for clothing, boots, food and money. She needed to return to supervise distribution and by 13 April 1927 she and her husband found themselves living at Maes-yr-haf ('summer meadows') in Trealaw, mid-Rhondda – a home which was to become a social and educational centre and where they were to remain for nearly 20 years. In 1928 Peter Scott (1890-1972) and his wife Lilian (d.1935) settled at

Bryn-mawr, a bleak town at the head of the eastern valley. They built up a co-operative which included a boot factory, pig and poultry farming and a furniture factory, *top left*, which achieved renown under Paul Matt (1901?-1987), the craft organiser for the many unemployed social clubs. In 1931 Quakers set up an Allotments Committee to encourage food production among the unemployed, *bottom*, distributing seed and garden implements at manageable prices – nearly 30,000 tons of seed potatoes and 267,000 spades and forks, apart from other help. And, *right*, is a reminder that the despair of unemployment and homelessness has been a continuing one.

Drawings co-ordinated by Anne Wynn-Wilson; embroidered by Win Prior, Sheena Millington and the Hemel Hempstead group

To provide mutual benefit relief and maintenance of Friends and their families

ASSURANCE

The true concern emerges as a gift from God a leading of the spirit which will not be denied

ACKWORTH
Old Scholars
Concern 1829

Joseph Rowntree
Samuel Tuke

Bradford 1832
London 1919
Dorking 1957

Quarterly Meeting at York
Then monthly and
Preparative meetings
established the

FRIENDS PROVIDENT
INSTITUTION

In 1828 Ackworth School suffered a severe fever epidemic which smote 183 of the pupils and staff and caused the death, at the age of 30, of Henry Brady, a popular master. He had married the previous year and his daughter, Henrietta, was born six months after his death. His widow, Hannah (1803-1882) is depicted, *left*, comforting his pupils. At the 1829 yearly meeting of British Quakers a collection was made for the widow and child. Joseph Rowntree and Samuel Tuke, *centre*, saw that this did not get to the root of the problem. Tuke had been among the first directors of the Yorkshire Fire & Life Insurance Co. (1824) and some unpublished writings of his grandfather, William Tuke, prompted him to study the fundamentals of life insurance. A number of provident societies had already come into being but, because they were not actuarily sound, had failed, causing more distress than they alleviated. In June 1831 a proposal to form a life insurance company was brought before the Money Matters Committee of Yorkshire Quakers. A month later it was agreed to go ahead; the first committee was held on 28 September and a prospectus issued two days later. In 1832 rules and regulations were approved, the introduction making it clear that insurance neither implied a distrust of Providence nor was in the nature of a lottery. The FPI started in one room over a baker's shop in Bradford, *bottom left*, which contrasts with its 1957 Dorking buildings, *bottom right*. When in 1920 FPI amalgamated with the Century Insurance Company, the first two non-Quaker directors were appointed. The number gradually increased and from 1983 it was no longer necessary that any Friends should be directors. In 1973 the company had changed its title to Friends Provident Life Office.

Designed and embroidered by Maggie Goodrich and the Epsom group

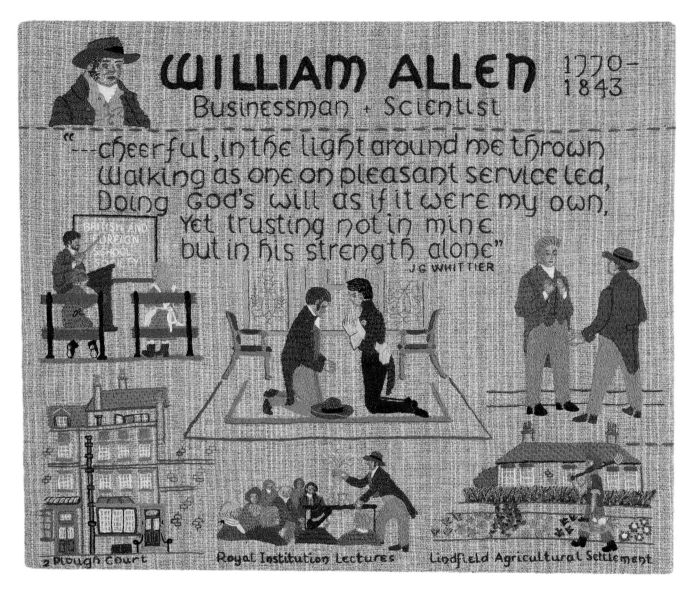

WILLIAM ALLEN 1770–1843
Businessman + Scientist

BRITISH AND FOREIGN SCHOOL SOCIETY

"...cheerful, in the light around me thrown
Walking as one on pleasant service led,
Doing God's will as if it were my own,
Yet trusting not in mine
but in his strength alone"
J G WHITTIER

2 Plough Court   Royal Institution Lectures   Lindfield Agricultural Settlement

E12 **William Allen**

William Allen (1770–1843), son of a Spitalfields silk weaver, had wide-ranging scientific, religious, social, educational and philanthropic interests. In 1792 he became an assistant at the Plough Court pharmacy, *bottom left*, a few years later becoming a partner in the firm, which later became Allen & Hanburys. From 1802 to 1826 he lectured in chemistry at Guy's Hospital; in 1807 he was elected a fellow of the Royal Society; and he was a founder member of the Mineralogical (1799), Geological (1807) and Pharmaceutical (1841) societies. In 1804 he began his Royal Institution lectures, *bottom centre*, and from 1808 he took an active part in the schools promoted by his fellow-Quaker Joseph Lancaster (1778–1838), whose vision was not matched by financial or administrative acumen. Allen was almost solely responsible for setting these schools, *middle left*, on a sound footing and the British & Foreign Schools Society (1813) was largely his creation. In 1821, while travelling in Sussex, he 'saw that a good system of education for the children of the labouring classes

was greatly needed in these districts' and began the agricultural colony at Lindfield, near Haywards Heath, *bottom right*, where he created a school farm and other training facilities for the children. With all this and more, he took an active part in Quaker activities and administration. He accompanied Stephen Grellet (*panel B5*) on an extended visit to the continent in 1818–9, where they saw the work of Daniel Wheeler (*panel F4*) and again met Czar Alexander I (whom they had seen in London in 1814). The Czar talked with them 'like old friends' on two occasions, questioning them about Friends' beliefs, discussing schools and prisons, and asking 'that we might have a little pause for mental retirement and inward prayer . . . a short but solemn time', *centre*.

Designed by Margery Levy; embroidered by the Salisbury group

George Fox in Derby gaol F1

After travelling in the east midlands since 1647 (*panel A1*) George Fox reached Derby in October 1650. He was told that at the church 'there was to be a great lecture that day and abundance of the officers of the army, and priests, and preachers were to be there'. Fox spoke to the congregation of 'the day of the Lord and the light within them'. He was taken before the magistrates 'and they put me in and out of the room from the first hour to the ninth hour at night in examinations'. He was then committed to prison for six months under the recently-passed Blasphemy Act. It was a tense time politically for, though the royalist Scots who had proclaimed Charles I's son king had just been routed at the battle of Dunbar, their threat remained. After six months in prison Fox was offered a captaincy in the Commonwealth army: when he refused, *top*, they thought this an exchange of politenesses, but when they found him firm he was hustled away into a dungeon 'amongst thirty felons in a lousy stinking low place in the ground, without any bed'. At the end

of August 1651 Cromwell's armies passed near Derby as it hastened to intercept the Scottish royalists at Worcester and 'Justice Bennet sent the constables to press me for a soldier seeing I would not accept of a command'. Again he refused. It was after the battle of Worcester in September that the uncrowned king fled back to the continent: next month Fox was released. He is shown, *centre*, writing. He had already appealed to merchants to deal justly: the market cross, *right*, with merchandise round it is a reminder that peace depends on economic justice. And, *bottom*, is an explanation of the origin of 'Quakers': early Friends referred to themselves as 'Children of Light' or 'Friends of Truth' and the description 'Religious Society of Friends' dates only from the late eighteenth century.

Designed by Taunton children and Anne Wynn-Wilson; embroidered by Margaret Gardner and Derby Friends

WILLIAM PENN + WILLIAM MEADE
were tried for preaching to an unlawful assembly

The jury refused to give a verdict against them although fined + locked up without food. Their stand established the right of Juries to give their verdict according to their convictions. 1670

F2 The Penn and Meade trial 1670

The Conventicle Act 1670 came into force on 10 May. It aimed, by the imposition of swingeing fines (five shillings for being at a conventicle, £20 for 'the preacher' and £40 for 'harbouring a conventicle'), to ruin dissenters. One-third of the fines, recoverable by distraint, were the perquisite of the common informer. The poet Andrew Marvell (1621-1678) called the act 'the quintessence of arbitrary malice'. It was the signal for renewed fierce persecution, as at Horsleydown (*panel C3*) and in many other places. On 14 August, the meeting house in Gracechurch Street, London, being locked against Friends, they met in the street. William Penn and William Meade were arrested and indicted for a riot – on the grounds that Penn had preached 'in Contempt of the King and of his Law to the great Terror and Disturbance of many of his Liege People and Subjects'. At the trial, before 10 justices, no witnesses could testify as to what Penn had said. After a vigorous defence by Penn, frequently interrupted by the bench, the jury brought in a verdict of 'Guilty of speaking in Gracious-street' – which was, of course, no offence. The recorder declared that the jury should not be dismissed until they brought in a verdict the court would accept. 'You are Englishmen', cried Penn to them, 'mind your Privilege; give not away your Right'. Despite the bench's threats the jury continued to return the same verdict until, a positive one being demanded, they returned 'Not guilty', for which they were fined and imprisoned for refusal to pay the fines. One of the jurors, Edward Bushell (1620-1694), brought an action for unjust imprisonment: judgment by the chief justice, Sir John Vaughan (1603-1674), no friend to nonconformity, in a speech of two or three hours' duration, established the rights of juries to bring in verdicts according to their conscience.

Designed by Joe McCrum; embroidered by Rachel Abbott and the Sevenoaks group

British Quakers protest to parliament against
THE SLAVE TRADE in 1783

God hath made of one blood
all nations of men for to dwell
upon the face of the earth

YEARLY MEETING — GRACECHURCH STREET

Slavery continues and is
a reproach to humanity

The slave trade F3

This panel is based on the oil painting 'Gracechurch Street meeting about 1770', the meeting house in which the yearly meetings of British Quakers were then held, men and women worshipping together, but at that time meeting separately for business. In 1772, when John Woolman (*panel A6*) was at the yearly meeting in London, its epistle expressed the hope that the slave trade might be 'utterly abolished'. American Quakers then made strenuous efforts to get Friends in Britain to give political aid to achieving that end. The American war of independence (1775-82) meant that the time was unpropitious but in 1783 the yearly meeting was ready to act, fully recognising that 'we must expect to meet with the greatest opposition of interested parties'. On 16 June it sent a petition to parliament signed by 273 Friends, urging that participation in the trade be forbidden absolutely: this was read aloud in the Commons next day. The chamber, *right*, whose panelling and galleries were the work of Christopher Wren (1632-1723), was destroyed in the fire of 1834. In 1783

Meeting for Sufferings (*panel A3*) appointed a committee which as a first step produced a well-argued pamphlet, *The case of our fellow-creatures, the oppressed Africans*, 12,000 copies being distributed, personally where possible, to people of influence. In 1787 the Quaker committee was replaced by a national one. The campaign, led by Thomas Clarkson (1760-1846), William Wilberforce (1759-1833) and Thomas Fowell Buxton (1786-1845), culminated in the 1807 act, which abolished the British slave trade, and the Emancipation Act 1833, which abolished slavery in the British dominions. Friends continued to support the British & Foreign Anti-Slavery Committee in its continuing campaigns to bring an end to slavery and indentured labour.

Designed by Margery Levy; embroidered at the Quaker Tapestry Exhibition centre at Kendal

Text within the embroidered panel:

DANIEL WHEELER was engaged in 1818 by Czar Alexander I to clear + drain 105,700 acres of the St Petersburg marshes.

God's love enableth me to call every country my country and every man my brother.

In later life he requested a ship that he might sail the South Seas to present the Quaker message.

F4 **Daniel Wheeler**

Following his meeting in 1814 with William Allen and Stephen Grellet (*panels E12, B5*), Czar Alexander I in 1817 asked them to find a Quaker agriculturist. As a result Daniel Wheeler and the young George Edmondson spent 14 years draining the marshes of Ochta, Volkova and Sushari, south of Petersburg, and introducing new methods of farming, *middle left*. Wheeler and his family, Edmondson, and on occasion a few others kept up regular Quaker meetings for worship, and it was in reflecting on one of these that Wheeler wrote in his journal the words quoted, *middle right*. The Czar, who used to visit the family informally, told William Allen and Stephen Grellet in 1819 of his appreciation of Wheeler's work and influence. In 1834, encouraged by Friends locally and nationally, Daniel Wheeler with his son Charles set sail for the southern hemisphere in the *Henry Freeling* (bought by Quakers in earnest of their support). On the voyage the ship met a severe storm, but was soon surrounded by a school of some 200 black fish 'about twelve feet long' which broke the

force of the waves and remained in position until the storm had abated, *bottom right*. For six months the Wheelers visited convict settlements and isolated Friends in Van Diemen's Land (Tasmania), often travelling with James Backhouse and George Washington Walker (*panel F20*), who accompanied them to Norfolk Island. From March 1835 to November 1836 the Wheelers visited extensively in the Pacific islands – Tahiti and other of the Society Islands, north to Honolulu and Hawaii, and back south to Tonga and New Zealand. They were struck by the demoralising effect on the native population of the European and American traders with their pressing sales of rum, muskets and gunpowder. After revisiting Australia they returned to England in May 1838.

Designed and embroidered by Anne Wynn-Wilson and the Bradford-on-Avon group

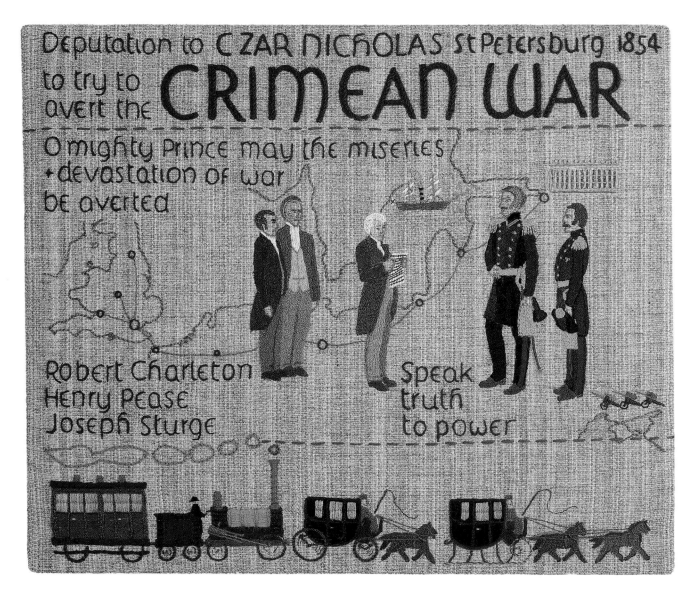

In the embroidery:

Deputation to CZAR NICHOLAS St Petersburg 1854 to try to avert the CRImEAn WAR

O mighty Prince may the miseries + devastation of war be averted

Robert Charleton
Henry Pease
Joseph Sturge

Speak truth to power

Delegation to the Czar 1854   F5

In December 1853 Joseph Sturge of Birmingham, concerned at the war fever fanned by an anti-Russian press, felt a concern for a Quaker delegation to go to the Czar Nicholas I. He brought this concern to Meeting for Sufferings (*panel A3*) on 6 January 1854: it prepared an address to the Czar and entrusted the delivery of it to Sturge, Henry Pease of Darlington and Robert Charleton of Bristol (*see biographical notes*). They left London at 8am on Friday 20 January and arrived at Petersburg (Petrograd) at 7pm on Thursday 2 February. As shown, *bottom*, they travelled by train to Königsberg, though they had to cross the ice-covered Vistula in a horse-drawn bus; they then travelled by coach to Riga; from Riga they changed the wheels of the coach for sledge runners because the snow was so deep. For some of the journey they needed seven horses to pull them through the drifts. They were well received in Petersburg. They saw the Russian chancellor on Monday and an interview with the Czar was arranged for Friday 10 February. Charleton

is shown, *left*, then Pease, then Sturge who read the address. Baron Nicolay, *right*, acted as interpreter. The delegation planned to return home immediately but the Czar pressed them to stay and meet his daughter, the Duchess of Leuchtenberg. When they did so the following Tuesday afternoon, the atmosphere, hitherto cordial, was formal and chilly. They believed that this must have been because the bellicose English papers had arrived: what they did not know was that diplomatic relations had been suspended by the British Foreign Office. They returned to meet the opprobrium of the British press. Henry Pease's great-granddaughter wrote, as Griselda Fox Mason, an account of the visit in *Sleigh ride to Russia* (1985).

Designed and embroidered by Mary Mason (Griselda Fox Mason) and family

The embroidered panel reads:

RELIEF WORK – BRITAIN "Our life is helping one another up with a tender hand"

Peterloo Massacre 1819 cotton workers ridden down by militia at a meeting for Parliamentary Reform are given refuge in the Friends Meeting House Manchester

1939 to 1945

Mount St Shelter

F6 Relief work: British Isles

On 16 August 1819 a large demonstration for parliamentary reform at St Peter's Field, Manchester, ended as the Peterloo massacre, when the Manchester Yeomanry Cavalry put down the protest at a cost of eleven killed and 400 injured. The nearby Friends meeting house in South Street 'served as a refuge for fugitive men, women and children, swept before the Yeomanry', *middle*. The new (1830) meeting house faced Mount Street and, *bottom*, under the vaulted ceiling of its basement some of the many activities are depicted. In 1938 local Quakers set up the Manchester & District Refugee Committee, with 2,250 German and Austrian refugees on its case books: a special fundraising feature was the annual exhibition and sale of refugee handicrafts, *bottom left*. In 1939 Manchester and Liverpool Quakers sponsored a scheme for the evacuation of children aged 3-12 years, *bottom, second from left*, to Yeland Manor in north Lancashire, where a school was established that became an educational and community experiment. The

meeting also provided a wartime air-raid shelter, *bottom right*. The Friends Ambulance Unit and Friends Relief Service (*panels F8, F7*) also worked in air-raid shelters in London's East End and other hard-hit areas. Before overseas work began, the Relief Service worked with those whose needs were not met by official schemes – they ran some 50 evacuation hostels for the elderly, 16 for families, a few for children, and five social welfare schemes. Among other examples of relief in the British isles are Friends' work during the Irish famine (*panel E8*) and allotment and other schemes for the unemployed (*panel E10*).

Designed by Margery Levy; embroidered by the Hardshaw East area monthly meeting and Cheshire area monthly meeting group

In the **RELIEF** of **SUFFERING**
we maintain the principle of impartial giving to all,
of whichever nation, race, creed or class are in need

1947 FSC·AFSC
shared the
Nobel Peace Prize

Quaker teams assess
situations + channel
aid through local
committees

Châlons Maternité
1914-7 3,789 patients

Caring for Displaced
Persons 1945-7

Training Centres 1938-45
Mount Waltham, Hampstead, + Spiceland, Devonshire
Relief workers need self-discipline + basic skills as well as
loving concern, building bridges of reconciliation

Relief work overseas   F 7

The red and black star, *left*, was adopted for Quaker relief work during and after the Franco-Prussian war (1870). Some 40 Friends, aged between 22 and 67, undertook the relief and made clear it was for non-combatants, whether French or German. This policy of impartiality has been consistently maintained. During and after the first world war some 2,000 volunteers were engaged in relief work in France, Holland, Russia, Poland, Austria and Germany: it is symbolised, *left*, by the Maison Maternelle at Chalons-sur-Marne. This was started in the unpropitious, gaunt, stone-floored Asile des Viellards and developed into an effective maternity home. In 1919 it was handed over to a French committee and in 1922 provided with new buildings. During and after the second world war there were 1,200 members of Friends Relief Service, some working on welfare schemes in this country and others in teams overseas - France, Germany, Poland and Austria: some members, *right*, are seen in their grey uniforms conferring with representatives of local social services. Much of the work in Germany was with displaced persons – Poles, Balts, Ukrainians, Yugoslavs and others brought to work compulsorily in German factories, and who at the end of the war could not or would not return home, *centre* – in 1948 there were still 212,000 in the British zone in need of immediate welfare as well as facing an uncertain future. In both world wars, as well as other times, many of those engaged in Quaker relief have not been themselves Friends, though likeminded in their attitudes. In 1947 British and American Quakers were awarded the Nobel Peace Prize for their relief work but, in accepting, made it clear that they saw their work in binding up some of the wounds of war as essentially a part of their peace testimony.

Designed by Joe McCrum; embroidered by the Wellington (Somerset) group

F8 **Friends Ambulance Unit**

In 1914 a group of Quakers set up the Friends Ambulance Unit for those pacifists who wanted to express their witness against war in corporate practical service. During the next five years 1,700 members (far from all of them Friends) worked in civilian and military hospitals in France, *left*, with French convoys, in hospital ships and on ambulance trains. There was also a section which worked in hospitals in England. In 1939 the older Friends who revived the Unit wisely left its running to 'young workers with young leaders among whom anyone over 35, at first even over 30, was rare'. Those members training in east London hospitals for ambulance work overseas found themselves, with the air raids from 7 September 1940, plunged into civilian relief work among bombed buildings *bottom right*, in shelters *middle right*, rest centres and Citizens Advice Bureaux. Similar work was undertaken on Merseyside and Tyneside. The Unit's work in the Middle East is depicted *bottom left*: in Syria 20 members ran five clinics under the supervision of

Syrian doctors. The arduous work of the China convoy in Szechwan (Sichuan) is shown *bottom centre* against a background of the Szechwan mountains. There were 139 members of the convoy, including Americans, Canadians, New Zealanders and 26 Chinese. In 1942, with 11 trucks lost in Burma, the age of petrol and plentiful spare parts was over, and that of charcoal-burning transport had arrived – lying under a lorry, attempting the repairs, was 'more the rule than the exception in west China'. The FAU worked also in Finland, north Africa, Ethiopia, India, Greece, Italy and north-west Europe. By 1946, when its work ended, there had been 1,300 members, Quakers and others. FAU was followed by FAU Post-war Service and FAU International Service, which closed in 1959.

Drawn and embroidered by the Sidcot group

In the embroidery:

SERVICE is love in action

The Visitors Centre Maze Prison

...listen to people on both sides and maybe help them to listen to one another

Quaker Cottage Belfast

Northern Ireland : Reconciliation   F9

Though 'Catholic' and 'Protestant' are longstanding labels in Northern Ireland, the divide, deeper and more complex, has been exacerbated by unemployment, dire poverty and overcrowding. On 12 August 1969 the annual march of the Londonderry apprentice boys led to the barricading of the Catholic Bogside area and the proclamation of 'free Derry'. There were immediate repercussions in Belfast and substantial contingents of British troops were drafted to Northern Ireland. Friends in Northern Ireland set up the forerunner of the Ulster Quaker Service Committee, which worked first of all on small practical tasks. After internment started in 1970 the Visitors Centre & Canteen, *centre*, at what became the Maze Prison, was begun in premises provided by government but run and originally wholly staffed by Quakers. Friends had been approached and asked to do this by relatives and supporters of internees. Welfare work developed with the setting up of an advice centre, the running of a minibus to help relatives with travel difficulties,

and the provision of child care facilities. In 1980 Quaker Cottage, *bottom*, was opened on a one-acre site on Black Mountain, west Belfast, initially as a rural centre for children from both cultures. It developed into a cross-community support centre which worked with mothers and children up to 11 years, providing a relaxed atmosphere in which mutual trust and friendships could be fostered. In 1982 Quaker House, Belfast, *top right*, was opened in University Avenue as a joint project of British and Irish Friends: this became a centre where men and women of all outlooks could meet in informal surroundings to listen to one another and discuss different perceptions and viewpoints.

Designed by Anne Wynn-Wilson; embroidered by Friends in Northern Ireland

Many thousand slaves found freedom travelling
The Underground Railroad

Following the North Star, they were
guided by many caring people
Levi Coffin
William Still
Thomas Garret
Harriet Tubman
Lucretia Mott *abolitionist*

"Thou shalt not deliver
unto his master the slave
which is escaped from
his master unto thee" DEUT 23:15

1786-1865
153 MILES

F 10 The Underground Railroad

When the United States Congress passed the Fugitive Slave Law 1793, empowering district or circuit judges or state magistrates to decide without jury the status of an alleged escaping slave, there was strong opposition in the northern states, some of whom passed personal liberty laws. As early as 1786 a group of Philadelphia Quakers had been noted as trying to help an escaping slave. After 1807, when the slave trade was abolished as far as Britain and her colonies were concerned, and especially after the Emancipation Act 1833, which abolished slavery throughout British colonies, Canada became a safe haven for these fugitives. The 'Underground Railroad' was started to help such escapes: the name arose because those involved in it so frequently spoke in railway terms – the tried routes were 'lines', the homes of sympathisers 'stations', those aiding the escape 'conductors' (*for details of the persons mentioned, not all of them Quakers, see biographical notes*). The main 'lines', *as shown*, were from Alabama, Arkansas and Kentucky through Illinois or Ohio to Canada, and from Georgia, the Carolinas and Virginia through Pennsylvania and New York or New England. There were narrow escapes. The sheriff's men, *bottom*, ride away while escaping slaves lie concealed in a farm cart. The demand of the southern states for more stringent federal legislation led to the Fugitive Slave Act 1850, but the severity of its measures led to abuse and was self-defeating – for the operations of the abolitionists increased, the 'Railroad' became even more efficient, and more states passed personal liberty laws. Legislation was repealed in 1864: estimates of the number of slaves who reached freedom vary from 40,000 to 100,000.

Designed and researched by Anne Wynn-Wilson and her students at Pendle Hill, Pennsylvania; drawings in bottom section by children of Wilmington High School; embroidered by the Armitage sisters

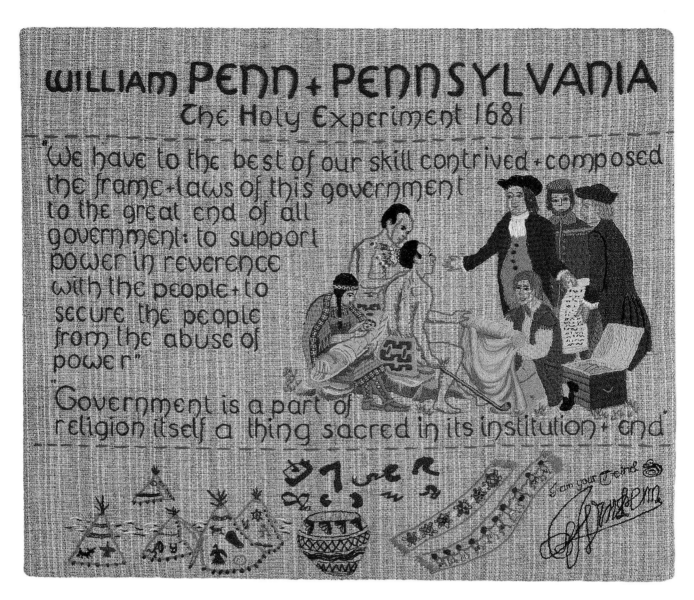

WILLIAM PENN + PENNSYLVANIA
The Holy Experiment 1681

"We have to the best of our skill contrived + composed the frame + laws of this government to the great end of all government: to support power in reverence with the people + to secure the people from the abuse of power"

"Government is a part of religion itself a thing sacred in its institution + end"

I am your friend
Penn

Penn and Pennsylvania F 11

By 1670 there were Quaker meetings the length of the eastern seaboard from Massachusetts to Virginia, and in the mid-1670s William Penn became one of three trustees for West Jersey, whose 1676 charter provided for full liberty of conscience. By 1681 some 1,400 Quakers had emigrated there. The following year Penn and 11 other Friends bought East Jersey. Meanwhile, Charles II wished to extinguish a debt of £16,000 which he owed to the estate of Penn's father, Admiral Sir William Penn (1621-1670), and in March 1681 he granted the son the substantial lands to the west of the Jerseys, pleasantly naming it Pennsylvania. Penn envisaged the colony as a 'holy experiment' based on democracy, religious toleration and peaceful institutions. It was a venture in Quaker government which was to last, at times very uneasily, for 70 years. The group, *centre*, is from the painting by Benjamin West (1738-1820) of 'the great treaty' under an elm tree at Shackamaxon between Penn and the Lenape Indians: that painting may be a work of historical imagination resulting from a series of

treaties on separate occasions. The panel shows, *right*, Penn and his fellow-Quakers offering gifts to the Indians, while, *bottom, middle*, are the signatures of nine Indian chiefs with, *further right*, a wampum belt and, *far right*, Penn's signature. Wampum, or tubular beads from river shells, were regarded as very precious by North American Indians, strings of them being used as currency, or belts woven from them serving as ceremonial gifts. From 1682 for two decades there was considerable emigration to Pennsylvania – probably for economic reasons more than because of persecution. The complaint of Welsh Friends (*panel F13*) echoed the experience of many English meetings and in 1686 the Quakers of Crefeld on the Rhine and of Griesheim in the Palatinate emigrated as a body.

Designed by Joe McCrum; embroidered by the Dorking & Horsham area monthly meeting group

Embroidered panel text:
LIVE ADVENTUROUSLY — Bring the whole of your daily life under the ordering of the spirit of Christ.

Nantucket whalers came to Milford Haven 1792

"When the war began we declared against taking any part of it..."

Gwyn ei byd yr oes a'u clyw,
Blessed is the generation that hears them.
Dangnefeddwyr, plant i Dduw
The peacemakers, the children of God

Waldo Williams 1904-71

F 12   **Nantucket and Milford Haven**

In the mid-seventeenth century some 20 families migrated from the North American mainland to Nantucket Island, off the coast of Massachusetts. These families developed a substantial whaling industry, *top right*, hunting the sperm whale as far as the Falkland Islands. Nantucket became virtually a Quaker colony of inter-related families. With the outbreak of the American war of independence they refused to support either side, with the result that the British ruined their trade by tariffs and the Americans shunned them as disloyal. Some of the whalers moved to Nova Scotia, others settled in Dunkirk: neither venture developed. Meanwhile, C.F. Greville, agent for the Hamilton estates in Pembrokeshire, had in 1790 secured parliamentary approval for the development of what would become Milford Haven (Aberdwyleddan). In 1792 some Nantucket families landed there, *centre left*, and a new town was built on American rectangular lines, *centre right*. A Quaker meeting house was opened in 1811, which saved the journey to the nearest meeting at

Haverfordwest. The whale-oil trade from Milford did not succeed and some of the Quakers returned to America while others left the Society, so that the meeting dwindled. There was a brief revival about 1908 and a steady increase from the 1950s. In 1953 Waldo Williams (1904-1971), *bottom right*, became a member of the meeting. He was a poet of some renown and a Plaid Cymru candidate for parliament. He was twice imprisoned for withholding tax in protest against the Korean war and was deeply concerned about the usurping of land for military use in rural Wales. He campaigned for the restoration to legal status of the Welsh language.

Designed by Wendy Gillett; embroidered by the Milford Haven group

FIDELITY to the TRUTH led hundreds of QUAKERS from persecution in the DOLGELLAU area to the NEW WORLD in the SEVENTEENTH century

Cader Idris

Brynmawr

Owen Lewis Tyddyn y garreg d. 1686

Pennsylvania

Dolgellau and Pennsylvania   F 13

In the seventeenth century there had been a flourishing yearly meeting for Wales: it was discontinued in 1797, for there remained only a few meetings, widely-scattered. By 1840 the only meetings in mid-Wales were Pales, Hay-on-Wye, Llanidloes, Llwyngwril and Tyddyn y Garreg. By 1850 all but the first two were closed; by 1870 Pales alone remained. Some 4,000 - 5,000 Welsh Quakers had emigrated to America by 1700, initially on account of persecution but perhaps increasingly in a search for more fertile land and better opportunities. The 'Welsh tract' in Pennsylvania perpetuates such names as Merion, Gwynedd, Bryn Mawr, Haverford, Radnor. The yearly meeting for Wales complained in 1698 of 'runnings to Pennsylvania [as the] cause of great weakening, if not total decaying, of some meetings'. The early Quaker families of Dolgellau, Merioneth, were of good standing in the neighbourhood (several of the men had been justices of the peace during the Commonwealth) and were of old Welsh princely stock. The five main

homes were Tyddyn y Garreg, Bryn-mawr, Dewisbren, Dolgun, Dolserau. The first of these, *centre*, was the home of Owen Lewis and, later, his son Lewis Owen: the yearly meeting for Wales was held here in 1685. Dewisbren, the home of Dorothy Owen (1751 -1793) and her parents, became the meeting place in the eighteenth century: a meeting house was built on their land in 1792. The figure, *left*, under arrest, is Rowland Ellis of Bryn-mawr; his house, though not used for meetings, was in the seventeenth century a centre for Friends from the neighbourhood and for visitors – it is of course not to be confused with Bryn-mawr in South Wales (*panel E10*).

Designed by Martyn Morley; embroidered by Ros Morley and the North Wales group

Quaker settlers arrived in New Zealand 1840

AOTEAROA

"This is our vision of the Peace that everyone needs in order to survive and flourish on a healthy abundant earth Stand up and be counted for what is no less than the affirmation of life and destiny of human kind."

Summer Gathering

F 14   New Zealand/Aotearoa

New Zealand Quakers in 1989 added to their title Aotearoa ('land of the long white cloud'), the Maori name for the country, as part of their commitment to the treaty of Waitangi, with its promise of partnership between the settlers and the indigenous Maoris. It was in 1840 that Britain's sovereignty was declared. Immediately, the New Zealand Company of the opportunist Edward Gibbon Wakefield (1796-1862) took possession of (and sold to settlers) vast tracts of land which the company purported to have bought from the Maoris: bitter fighting ensued. In these tense circumstances Thomas (1818-1903) and Jane (d.1900) Mason of York settled at Taita in 1841. Because of the unrest they moved in 1846 to Van Diemen's Land (*panel F20*) but returned in 1851, establishing a fruit orchard. He also bought and rented from the Maoris substantial acreage for sheep farming. Owing to a surveying error and a change of Maori leader 2,000 sheep were taken from him for alleged arrears of rent. Mason made clear the actual position but declined to use force to regain his flock

which, a few months later, were returned, *top right*. The patterned border, *top, far right*, is a Maori design, its wording 'Tutu ana puaha' denoting the power of oratory to stir up the hearers. During the first world war Auckland Quakers began a practice of taking flowers each week to prisoners in Mount Eden gaol, *top left*. In 1976 the Wanganui Friends Educational Settlement was founded on land previously part of Friends School (1920-69) as a community of about a dozen families and individuals and also to provide a centre for study, retreat, and gatherings of various kinds, *bottom*. In front of the buildings is a kowhai tree. The pohutukawa tree, with flax and a kiwi at its base, *left*, flowers at Christmas: a tui (parson bird) is eating honey from the flax flowers.

Designed by Karol London; embroidered by Brenda Meadows and Friends throughout New Zealand

Pierre Ceresole (1879-1973) was a Swiss engineer who became a Quaker in 1936. During the first world war he was resolute in opposing violence of any kind, going to gaol rather than pay the military tax. In 1920, at a conference at Bilthoven, Holland, it was agreed to form an international team to help villagers in northern France rebuild their farms. This was the beginning of International Voluntary Service – Pierre Ceresole's vision of 'an army of men without hatred' who would replace conscription by voluntary service. The number of volunteers increased and in 1931-2 they worked with the South Wales unemployed at Bryn-mawr (*panel E10*), making a swimming pool. Jack Hoyland (1887-1957), after 12 years as a missionary in India, was for 24 years a lecturer at Woodbrooke (*panel B6*). He too had worked with the unemployed in South Wales and was always concerned to stress that work done *with* people was of far greater value than work done *for* them, even if it involved some loss of efficiency. He wrote out of his experience *Digging with the unemployed* (1934) and

Digging for a new England (1936). After the second world war the work camp movement gained fresh impetus and from 1962 three-week tripartite work-and-study projects began to be held, bringing together young Americans, Russians and British. Gradually the emphasis on 'pick and shovel' camps, *middle*, gave way to camps preoccupied with the physically or mentally disabled, the elderly, and others in particular need, *bottom*, so that the description 'international social projects' came to be seen as more accurate.

Designed and embroidered by the Gloucester & Nailsworth area monthly meeting group

TRUE PEACE cannot be dictated, it can only be built in co-operation between all peoples: Yearly Meeting 1943

Quaker United Nations Offices: Geneva, New York.
Quaker Council for European Affairs·Brussels.

School of Peace Studies University of Bradford established 1972.

Every step to diminish fear is a step towards peace.

Co-operation is better than conflict.

F 16   **Peace embassies**

'The two mules', *bottom*, has long been a popular peace poster – and since 1900 Quakers have seen posters as important in peace witness. Friends have also been concerned to build the institutions of peace. Carl Heath (1869-1950), secretary of the National Peace Council, became a Quaker in 1916. The following year, at a conference at Skipton, Yorkshire, he pleaded for 'the planting of a Quaker embassy in every European capital'. This vision was translated into Quaker centres, including Paris, Berlin and Geneva. During the second world war a London centre was opened and, following the establishment of the United Nations, Quakers worldwide received recognition as a non-governmental agency. This led to the opening of Quaker House, New York and the Quaker United Nations Programme there and at Geneva. In the 1950s British Friends began a series of seminars for diplomats, believing that as they met in informal surroundings deeper relationships would be built up and mutual confidence increased. The panel depicts,

left, any small international gathering arranged in the New York or Geneva centre. With the development of the European Economic Community, a Quaker Council for European Affairs was set up and a centre at Brussels opened. Early in 1970 British Friends agreed to explore the possibility of establishing a university chair of peace studies, such as existed in Norway and the United States. By the end of the year the University of Bradford was willing to do so. The vice-chancellor and Cardinal Heenan jointly sponsored an appeal for half the endowment, the university meeting the other half. By 1973 the first occupant of the chair was at work, with graduate students admitted in October 1974 and undergraduates a year later, *right*.

Designed by Joe McCrum and Anne Wynn-Wilson; embroidered by the Chichester area monthly meeting and Lewes area monthly meeting group

In the image:

QUAKER VIGILS FOR PEACE
Trafalgar Square 1980

IT IS BETTER TO SHARE — PEOPLE NEED WATER NOT BOMBS — ARMS SALES — WITNESS FOR PEACE — PEACE BEGINS IN THE HEARTS of the PEOPLE — bread not bombs — UNARMED TRUTH — QUAKER VIGIL FOR PEACE — DISARM FOR LIFE — PEACE ONLY THROUGH THE WILL OF PEOPLE

We utterly deny all outward war + strife + fightings with outward weapons, for any end whatever.. This is our testimony to the whole world

This panel depicts a witness for peace in Trafalgar Square in May 1980. It was held during the yearly meeting of British Quakers and a thousand Quakers walked from Friends House in Euston Road two by two, in an exceedingly long crocodile. They were in groups of 40, badged and bannered fore and aft and, such was the almost military precision of the organisation that, as six o'clock struck from St Martin in the Fields, the last group reached the Square and the supporting group of saffron-robed Buddhists graciously ceased their drumming, as essential to their witness in the streets of London as silence is to the Quakers. It was neither the first nor the last such occasion. Following Pope Paul VI's 1966 call to prayer for peace in Vietnam, many Quakers were among the 100 people who, on Human Rights day, met on the steps of St Martin in the Fields in silent prayer; others joined similar groups throughout the country. On many other occasions Quakers nationwide have held vigils, increasingly joining in an ecumenical witness. In 1968 the yearly meeting of British Quakers agreed to hold a witness for peace outside Westminster Abbey. On an August Sunday afternoon some 600-700 Friends were joined by the dean and two members of the chapter and, after a 45-minute silent gathering, filed slowly into the abbey for a final time of quiet and prayer 'for the peace of all mankind'. To make clear the purpose of this silent witness to the many visitors passing between Victoria Street and Parliament Square, young Friends on the edge of the group distributed 2,000 leaflets which dealt not only with the need for peace but for racial justice, help to poorer nations and 'a new standard of values, a non-violent revolution'.

Designed by Joe McCrum; embroidered by Catherine Walton and the Uxbridge group

5th WORLD CONFERENCE
Meeting on three sites_

In Spirit and in Truth, Faith in Action.

1991

Netherlands
Honduras
Kenya

Building bridges between our divisions
I reach out to you. will you reach out to me?
With all of our voices + all of our visions
Friends we could make such sweet harmony.

F 18 **World Conference 1991**

By the end of the seventeenth century there was a yearly meeting in Amsterdam for the Netherlands, Friedrichstaad and Dantzig, six yearly meetings stretching from New England to North Carolina, and annual gatherings of Quakers in Jamaica, Barbados, and Nevis. During the eighteenth century the meetings on the continent and in the West Indies died out, but new groups of like-minded people round Congénies in the south of France and Pyrmont in Germany (*panel C5*) were 'discovered' by British and American Friends. During the nineteenth century these too died out. There were a few Friends in Norway and Denmark; and missionary work had led to small Quaker communities in Syria and Palestine, mid-India, China, Japan, Madagascar and Pemba. But in 1900 Quakerism was still primarily Anglo-Saxon. During the first world war there was concern that Quakers worldwide should re-examine the implications of their peace testimony and an All Friends Conference (1920) was held in London: of the 936

representatives, 890 were from Britain, Ireland and North America and only 46 from the rest of the world. Later world conferences were held in 1937, 1952 and 1967. At the fifth world conference (1991) there were 1,027 representatives, 490 from Britain, Ireland and North America and 537 from the rest of the world: to make the occasion manageable it was, *as shown here*, held in three places, but each conference had world and not merely regional representation. In 1994 there were some 300,000 Quakers worldwide – about 100,000 in the United States, 100,000 in Kenya, and over 50,000 in Central and South America. The twentieth century has therefore seen not only the growth of theological but also the recognition of cultural diversity (*see also final panel*).

Designed by Anne Wynn-Wilson; embroidered by Rugby Friends

A few Dutch Quakers were in Cape Town in the 1720s; later, meetings for worship were held there by the Nantucket whalers (*panel F12*); James Backhouse and George Washington Walker (*panels F20, D 8*) travelled widely in South Africa from 1838 to 1840; there were other occasional visits of British Friends. An early emigrant was the London Quaker James Butler (1854-1923) who had gone in 1876 for his health and settled at Cradock, as did his brother Charles (1864-1949), *bottom right*. In 1891 James began the *Midland news* as a newspaper of independent comment and increasingly radical criticism (which his brother did not share). During the Anglo-Boer war (1899-1902) Quakers engaged in relief work in the camps to which Boer women and children had been moved, *left*. William H.F. Alexander (1855-1941) had a particular concern that the Boer family bibles, *bottom left*, looted by British soldiers, should be returned to their owners and through his patient work 130 were restored. After the shootings at Sharpeville in 1960, when police

opened fire on an African crowd, killing 67 and wounding 186, Olive Gibson of Birmingham worked in Johannesburg from 1961 to 1984 under the South African Friends' Quaker Service Fund. The centre was there to help African families, especially from Soweto, to cope with problems such as the imprisonment of the breadwinner or of children, *middle right; bottom centre*. In the first quarter of 1967, 367 families or individuals were helped, involving 860 office interviews and 340 visits. In 1988 the Quaker Peace Centre in Cape Town, *centre*, was opened to promote peace education, community and economic development, and conflict management: in 1996 there was a staff of 34 as well as 21 community mediators.

Designed by Avril Brown; embroidered by the Hampstead area monthly meeting group and Friends in South Africa

F 20 **Tasmania**

The American Revolution deprived Britain of a place of exile for her convicts. New South Wales was seen as an admirable alternative and, between 1788 and 1841, it received over 83,000 convicts. By 1790 Norfolk Island, far out in the Pacific, had been developed as a subsidiary settlement. The first British settlement in Van Diemen's Land (from 1853, Tasmania) was in 1804. Most of the first settlers, both free and convict, had been transferred from Norfolk Island. Elizabeth Fry had from 1818 concerned herself with the conditions of women convicts alike on the voyage and on arrival (*panel E6*) and other British Quakers also became concerned at the situation. The panel depicts, in front of the palings, George Washington Walker, *left*, and James Backhouse, *right*. They sailed from England in September 1831 and, after a brief time in Cape Town, arrived in Van Diemen's Land in June 1832. Their aims were both religious and practical – to preach the gospel to scattered settlers, to investigate the penal system, to find out how aborigines were being treated, and to promote temperance. They visited most of the settlers, convict and free, in Van Diemen's Land and the convict settlements in New South Wales, and Norfolk Island and West Australia, leaving on 12 February 1838 for Mauritius and South Africa (*panel F19*). They were very briefly in South Australia. Neither man was robust yet, of the 4,260 miles travelled in Australia and Mauritius, 3,000 were on foot, 1,000 on horseback, and the small remainder by coach or rowboat. Backhouse made daily use of his botanical knowledge (*panel D8*) to identify flora and note botanical classification, thus providing one of the earliest reference books on Tasmanian flora.

Designed by Martin Aptisis; embroidered by Friends in Tasmania

Canada   F21

Quakers migrated to Canada towards the end of the eighteenth century. The first meeting was established in 1801 at Yonge Street, north of Toronto, the 1810 meeting house, *top right*, being still in use (1997). Initially, most Quaker communities were in southern Ontario, but by 1890 there were a number of Friends in the Canadian west. Alma Dale (1855?-1930) twice travelled extensively through Manitoba and as far as British Columbia, drawn by her cream horses, *bottom left*, to support and encourage isolated Friends and help establish Quaker meetings. In 1924 Toronto Friends started to run boys' and girls' clubs: the need for a summer holiday camp for them led to the opening in 1930 of Camp Neekhaunis ('place of friendly meeting'), 90 miles north of the city, on the shores of Georgian Bay. The campsite, *centre*, fully used during the summer months, has served also as a meeting point for Canadian Quakers. From 1899 Canadian Friends have had links with the Dukhobors, an eighteenth century much-persecuted Russian sect. In 1898, when the

Czar allowed them to emigrate, British Quakers rapidly raised the needed £16,000, and in 1899 7,500 of them reached Canada, where they set to cultivate 270,000 acres in Saskatchewan. That summer Eliza Varney of Bloomfield, Ontario, volunteered to run a dispensary in a tent. The following year she returned with Nellie Baker who used a second tent to teach school to the children, *left*. Canadian Quakers have also been concerned for the land rights and cultural heritage of native peoples: the salmon, *middle right*, is the symbol of the Micmac nation. Hundreds of school orchards, *bottom right*, have been cultivated in Mexico as a result of a project of Friends in Victoria, British Columbia, to teach gardening to Mexican school children.

Designed by Bette Dewhurst and Ann Nichols; embroidered by Ann Nichols and Friends throughout Canada

FRIENDS in the NETHERLANDS

Jewish Children hidden in Quaker homes

LAURA'S HOUSE 40

Prinsengracht

1940-45

The POLLATZ family house Haarlem

"God heeft mensen nodig": God needs people.

F 22   The Netherlands 1940-5

The seventeenth-century Quaker meetings in
Holland had died out by 1800 and the rebirth of
Quakerism in the Netherlands belongs to the 1920s.
Dutch students at Woodbrooke (*panel B6*) who had
become familiar there with Quaker worship and
practice returned home and began to meet for
worship with others likeminded. A yearly meeting
was established in 1931. Manfred (1886-1964) and
Lili (d. 1946) Pollatz were German Quakers, living in
Saxony. They were teachers and, following the rise to
power of Hitler in 1933, Manfred resigned his post
because he would not conform to Nazi regulations.
In 1934 they brought their young family to Holland
and took into their new home in Haarlem six or
seven German refugee children whom they educated
with their own four. Soon the number of their guests
rose to 14, all but one Jewish or part-Jewish. Few had
parents able to pay for their keep and in 1936, when
Manfred's pension was stopped, finance became
precarious. Nevertheless, their Home School,
recognised but not financially supported by the

Dutch Ministry of Home Affairs, created 'a rich
intellectual and spiritual atmosphere' for the
children, though the living conditions were spartan.
In February 1939 Dutch Quakers opened a relief
office in Amsterdam to help some of the many
German refugees fleeing to Holland. In May 1940,
with the German invasion, the Pollatz family took
into their home children and others whose lives
were in danger. In consequence Manfred was taken
to a concentration camp in 1943. In 1945, when a
gathering of the yearly meeting was again possible,
its epistle contained these words: 'For five years we
have been living under an oppression such as cannot
be realised by those who have not experienced it,
and now it has fallen from us suddenly. God gives us
and the whole world again fresh chances'.

*Designed by Anne Wynn-Wilson; embroidered by the
Netherlands group*

The world family of Friends

In 1654 the first publishers of Truth (*panels B4, C1*) travelled not only the length of Britain and Ireland but to the continent of Europe, the West Indies, and the eastern seaboard of North America. The many meetings they established were grouped into yearly meetings, which had a 'heavenly correspondence' with one another by the exchange of epistles and were united in one family by the visits of Friends travelling in the ministry. From the 1820s individual Friends and whole communities crossed the Alleghenies into Ohio and Indiana, moving steadily west and south-west with the advancing frontier. The great religious revival of the 1860s also had an impact on American Quakerism, particularly in the middle and far west: by the 1880s many meetings began to have paid pastors and a set service with hymns and a prepared sermon. Many Friends, however, continued the traditional unprogrammed worship in silent waiting. Thus, *left and right of the tree*, there are Friends' churches and Friends' meeting houses. At the second world conference

(1937, *panel F18*) the Friends World Committee for Consultation was set up to foster greater understanding between Quakers of different traditions. After the second world war it started a pattern of triennial meetings and of encouraging intervisitation and publications. The oak tree, *centre*, is a symbol, like the prism, of unity in diversity, of a wealth of branches rooted in one source. The drawings, *bottom*, serve as a reminder that it is through personal friendships that bridges are built between those of different traditions.

Designed by Anne Wynn-Wilson, drawings of 'Me and my friends' being by children in the countries named; embroidered by Anne Wynn-Wilson, Win Prior and 'an enormous number of people' in Switzerland, North America and Britain

Appendix A: Biographical notes

These notes do not pretend to give a balanced overview of the individuals included: they aim to do no more than add some depth to the reference in the relevant Tapestry panel or panels. Biographical information contained in the explanatory text to the panel itself is not, in general, repeated here. Effort has been made to provide fuller information about lesser known persons than about those for whom other reference works are more readily available.

Alexander I (1777-1825), emperor of Russia 1801-25, had been brought up in the freethinking atmosphere of Catherine II's court and had imbibed the philosophy of Rousseau. When in London in 1814 the emperor expressed a wish to attend a Quaker meeting and, accompanied by William Allen, worshipped at Westminster. On returning to Russia he asked for a Quaker agriculturist, resulting in the long service there of Daniel Wheeler *qv*. In 1819, when William Allen and Stephen Grellet were in Petersburg, the emperor had two long conversations with them. *Panels B5, E12, F4*

Austin, Ann (d. 1665) in late 1655 accompanied Mary Fisher *qv* to Barbados – being the first Quakers to reach the Americas. In July 1656 they arrived in Boston, Massachusetts, where they were searched, imprisoned, and after five weeks sent back to Barbados. They returned to England separately in the winter of 1656/7. She then settled in London, was imprisoned in 1659, and died during the great plague. *Panel B2*

Backhouse, James (1794-1861), son of a Darlington banker and first cousin to Jonathan Backhouse *qv*, became a nurseryman in York. At 18, through the ministry of Stephen Grellet, he sensed that he would be called to service in a far-off country: three years later he saw this as Australia. Later he met Elizabeth Fry, visited Newgate prison with her, and became concerned for prisoners who were transported. With George Washington Walker *qv* he visited between 1831 and 1840 Tasmania, parts of mainland Australia, Mauritius and South Africa. In 1853 and 1860 he visited Norway. *Panels D8, F20*

Backhouse, Jonathan (1779-1842) came of a family of yeoman farmers in Yealand, north Lancashire. His grandfather, James (1721-1798), had moved to Darlington as a flax-dresser and linen manufacturer and in 1774 established the family bank which in 1896 became part of Barclays. Jonathan Backhouse married in 1811 Hannah Chapman Gurney and from 1830 was associated with the Norwich banking house of Gurneys & Co. He was a warm supporter of the British & Foreign Bible Society, the anti-slavery movement, and the welfare of Australian aborigines. *Panel E3*

Baker, Sarah Martha (1887-1917) was the daughter of a London Quaker engineer. From childhood she had an intense love of flowers. She took an honours degree in chemistry at University College, London, subsequently becoming a lecturer there. Her particular study was the biochemistry of plants but her research ranged from the ecology of seaweeds to the breadmaking properties of substitutes for wheaten flour. She was elected a fellow of the Linnean Society in 1914. *Panel D8*

Barclay, Robert I (1648-1690), son of Colonel David Barclay (1610-1686) of Ury, near Aberdeen, was educated in France, then returning home. He became a Quaker about 1666, shortly after his father. He suffered imprisonment at Montrose (1672) and Aberdeen Tolbooth (1676). In 1669 he had married Christian Molleson (1647-1723). In 1677 he visited Holland with George Fox and William Penn *qqv*. His scholarly background and systematic thinking were of particular service to early Quakerism and, besides the *Apology*, he wrote a number of other books and pamphlets. His eldest son, **Robert Barclay II (1672-1747)**, accompanied his father to London twice before he was 20, meeting George Fox *qv* and many other eminent Friends, and members of the court at Windsor. He succeeded his father as laird of Ury and was also a ministering Friend of some note. The second son, **David Barclay (1682-1769)**, moved to London as a young man. His business was based largely on the American trade. He married into the Freame family of Quaker goldsmiths and bankers, and his eldest son, James (1708-1766), became in 1736 a partner in the banking concern which ultimately became Barclays Bank. *Panels B4, A9 (RB II), D2 (DB)*

Bartram, John (1699-1777) was born near Philadelphia, Pennsylvania, his parents having emigrated from Derbyshire in 1682. In 1708 he inherited a farm from an uncle and on this he worked for most of his life. He soon began to travel in search of plants and to collect and propagate seeds, and was put in touch with Peter Collinson *qv*, forming a lifelong association. In 1728 he bought five acres of ground on the Schuykill river and developed the first botanical garden in America. He was a founder member of the American Philosophical Society (1743) and his extensive travels, described in *Observations* (1751) and *A description* (1766), laid the foundations of our knowledge of American flora. His Quaker membership was terminated in 1758 on account of his liberal theological views but he maintained his regular attendance at his local Friends' meeting. *Panel D8*

Beale, Benjamin, who invented the bathing machine about 1750 (but did not patent it), was the husband of Elizabeth (1714?-1806): she was convinced of Friends' principles also about 1750 and became a recorded minister in the Society a few years later. She was given to reproving the worldly attire of some Quaker visitors to Margate and they complained of her severity. Her husband is a more shadowy figure about whom more information is desirable. *Panel D9*

Bellers, John (1654-1725), the son of a wealthy London Quaker grocer, became a cloth merchant in the city and an active member of the Meeting for Sufferings (*panel A3*). He married in 1686 Frances Fettiplace of Coln St Aldwyn, Gloucestershire, her father being lord of the manor. The Bellers settled at The Grange, Chalfont St Peter, Buckinghamshire, formerly the home of Isaac and Mary

Penington *qqv*. In 1701, on the death of Frances' mother, they moved to her Gloucestershire home. In 1718 he was elected a fellow of the Royal Society. *Panel E2*

Bradshaw, George (1801-1853), timetable printer, was born in Salford, Lancashire, apprenticed to a Manchester engraver, and in 1820 set up business in Belfast, returning to Manchester two years later. In 1838 or 1839 he first issued *Bradshaw's railway companion* and in 1841 the larger *Bradshaw's railway guide* which, published monthly, ousted the *Companion* in popularity. Its last issue (no. 1521) was in June 1961. Bradshaw had become a Quaker about 1820: his main concern was for international peace and he was one of the promoters of the first international peace congress (Paris 1849). In 1853 he died at Christiana (Oslo), having contracted cholera while visiting a former Manchester acquaintance there. *Panel D7*

Burrough, Edward (1634-1662), a farmer of Underbarrow, near Kendal, and preacher among the seekers, became a Quaker in 1652 and from 1654 was one of the foremost Quaker preachers in London. With Francis Howgill *qv* he travelled extensively in Ireland in 1655. He was a prolific writer, being author of some 80 tracts. He died in Newgate prison. *Panel B4*

Cash, Newman (1792-1866), son of a Coventry stuff weaver, became a stuff merchant in Leeds. He was a founder director of the Friends Provident Institution (1832), an original promoter of the Leeds & Selby Railway (1834), a founder member of Leeds Peace Association (1842), and a director of the Leeds Northern (from 1854, North Eastern) Railway until his death. *Panel D6*

Charleton, Robert (1809-1872) came of a Bristol Quaker family and was a pin manufacturer. Concerned for the education of the poor, he built and maintained schools in and about Kingswood, east of the city. After his 1854 visit to Russia with Joseph Sturge and Henry Pease *qqv*, he returned there in 1858 on a Quaker delegation to present 'A plea for liberty of conscience': the group also visited Finland and Denmark. He actively promoted the establishment of the Friends Foreign Mission Association (1868). *Panel F5*

Clark, Benjamin of George Yard, Lombard Street, London, was one of the two principal printers and publishers for Friends between 1674 and 1683, the other being Andrew Sowle (1628-1695). Of all the early printers for Friends, Clark appears to have had the broadest outlook and the most scholarly connections. Among his authors were Robert Barclay, Thomas Ellwood, Thomas Lawson, Isaac Penington, and William Penn *qqv*. He was the London publisher of the first (Latin) edition of Barclay's *Apology*, printed in Holland (1676). He issued over 60 books and pamphlets for Friends, but his relationship with the Quaker committee responsible for publications was not always harmonious and he does not appear to have printed for Friends after 1683. He dealt in other literature as well, and there is evidence that he published school books until at least 1698. *Panel B4*

Cock, Luke (1657?-1740), a butcher at Staithes, on the Yorkshire coast north of Whitby, became a Quaker some time after his marriage and for his last 37 years was a ministering Friend. He is best, and almost solely, known for his 'Weeping cross' sermon at York in 1721 (printed in William Charles Braithwaite, *Second period of Quakerism*, 1919, pp. 551-3), describing unaffectedly his difficulties in accepting Friends' testimonies on truthfulness and integrity, his wife (who was later convinced) at one time crying 'We'se all be ruined: what, art thou going stark mad to follow these silly Quakers.' *Panel D5*

Coffin, Levi (1798-1877) was born in New Garden, North Carolina, but later moved to Ohio, where his home was the meeting point of three 'Underground Railroad' 'lines' from Kentucky. In 1847 he moved to Cincinatti as agent for the Free Labor Association, opening a depot for the sale of goods free from slave labour. More than 3,000 fugitive slaves passed through his hands. *Panel F10*

Collinson, Peter (1693-1768) was the son of a Cumberland Quaker who had settled in London as a wholesale woollen-draper. This prosperous business was continued by Peter and his brother and gave him sufficient leisure and fortune to pursue his botanical studies, which had begun at an early age. The extensive business trade overseas enabled him to secure rarities of all kinds through sea captains sailing to all parts of the world. He planted a large garden at Peckham in which he germinated and cultivated the seeds and plants he acquired, but in 1749 moved to Mill Hill. In 1728 he became a fellow of the Royal Society and his wide circle of correspondents and friends included John Bartram and John Fothergill *qqv*. *Panel D8*

Curtis, William (1747-1799) was born at Alton, Hampshire, a member of an extensive Quaker family, many of whom, over several generations, were apothecaries and botanists. He became demonstrator in botany at the Company of Apothecaries, London, and developed a botanical garden and library at Lambeth Marsh. His greatest work was his *Flora Londinensis* (3 vol., 1774-87) but he is perhaps best known for *Curtis's botanical magazine* which, started in 1787, is still (1997) being published. His Quaker membership was formally ended in 1791 but had effectively ceased long before that. *Panel D8*

Dalton, John (1766-1844) came of a Cumberland Quaker family. He and his brother conducted the Friends' school at Kendal from 1781 to 1793, when he was appointed professor of mathematics and natural philosophy at the New College, Manchester. In 1787 he began a meteorological diary which he kept up for 57 years, with 200,000 observations: his *Meteorological observations and essays* (1793) was followed by a number of other works on the subject. By 1804 his work in chemistry which resulted in the atomic theory had made good progress and in 1807 he delivered his views in lectures before the universities of Glasgow and Edinburgh, the first publication of the theory being in 1808. He was elected a fellow of the Royal Society in 1822. *Panel D10*

Darby, Abraham I (1678-1717) was the son of a Quaker family in Dudley, Worcestershire, and was apprenticed to a maltmill maker in Birmingham. In 1699 he set up business in Bristol, soon extending it to include brass casting and experimenting with cast iron. In 1704 he went to Holland to study their methods and in 1707 patented his invention for casting bellied iron pots in sand. This opened up a new field with an almost inexhaustible domestic market, and it was with this background that he moved to Coalbrookdale in 1708. *Panel D4*

Darby, Abraham II (1711-1763), son of Abraham I *qv* was a minor when his father died: until he reached his majority in 1732 the partnership was held by his mother and two other Friends, one being his brother-in-law. Abraham II, when he took over the management, began a policy of expansion to meet the increasing demand for pig iron and cast iron goods. *Panel D4*

Darby, Abraham III (1750-1789), son of Abraham II *qv*, took over the management of the Dale works when he was 18. In 1776, when considering the consolidation of the works, he made extensive property purchases and secured the lease of minerals throughout the area. He also saw considerable expansion of the Cornish trade. *Panel D4*

Dyer, Mary (d. 1660) came of an Essex family, though born in London. She married in 1633 William Dyer and they emigrated to Boston, Massachusetts, where he became a milliner. In 1637, when Anne Hutchinson was excommunicated by her church in Boston for heresy, Mary Dyer stepped from her seat and went with her. They all moved to more tolerant Rhode Island. By 1656, when Mary Dyer returned to England, she had embraced Quaker principles. In 1658 the Massachusetts legislature enacted the penalty of banishment on pain of death upon any Quaker entering the colony and in June 1659 she and two men Friends came into the colony 'Boston's bloody laws to try'. They were banished, returned, and sentenced to death. The two men were hanged but she was reprieved. She returned in May 1660 and was hanged on Boston Common. *Panel B2*

Eddington, *sir* Arthur Stanley (1882-1944) was the only son of Arthur Henry Eddington (1850-1884), headmaster of Stramongate School, Kendal, from 1878 until his early death from typhoid. ASE was senior wrangler at Cambridge and was appointed in 1906 chief assistant to the astronomer royal at Greenwich. In 1913 he became Plumian professor of astronomy at Cambridge and the following year director of the university observatory. He was elected a fellow of the Royal Society in 1914. His many books include *Stellar movements and the structure of the universe* (1914) and *The mathematical theory of relativity* (1923) – Einstein accepted him as his best interpreter. More popular works were *The nature of the physical world* (1927) and *The expanding universe* (1933). He was president of the Physical Society, the Royal Astronomical Society, and the International Astronomical Union. He was chairman of the National Peace Council from 1941 to 1944. He must not be confused with his first cousin Arthur J. Eddington (1886-1943) of Norwich, historian of

Quaker Norfolk and clerk of Meeting for Sufferings from 1938 to 1943. *Panel D10*

Edmondson, Thomas (1792-1851), inventor of the railway ticket, was born into a Lancaster Quaker family. After his Carlisle business of cabinet-making and upholstery went bankrupt he became in 1837 stationmaster at Milton (later Brampton Junction) station on the Newcastle & Carlisle Railway. Finding no satisfactory system of receipts, he started writing pre-numbered tickets, later using card and simple printing. In 1841, after two years with the Manchester & Leeds Railway, he set up business as a ticket printer: within six years 74 of the 80 railway companies in Britain were using Edmondson tickets. The firm remained until 1960. His brother **George Edmondson (1798-1863)** was, after schooldays at Ackworth, apprenticed to William Singleton *qv* at his school at Loxley, near Sheffield until 1818, when he joined Daniel Wheeler *qv* in his work in Russia. In 1821 he married Singleton's daughter Anne (1798?-1863) but, on account of her health, they had to leave Russia in 1825 and return to England. He then built up Tulketh Hall School, near Blackburn. In 1847 he opened Queenwood College, near Stockbridge, Hampshire (*panel C7*), taking over the 400 acres and palatial buildings erected by Robert Owen (1771-1858) for his Harmony Hall community experiment: Queenwood combined a boys' school and an agricultural college for young men and was a pioneer establishment in the teaching of science. *Panels D7, F4 (GE)*

Elam, Gervase (1681-1771) moved in 1693 from Heath, near Halifax, to Leeds where he became a prosperous clothier. His six sons who reached adulthood expanded the business or branched out into new fields. By the 1740s the eldest, John (1721-1789), had set up as a tobacco importer, his brother Emmanuel (1729-1796) joining him as apprentice, while three more brothers, Gervase II (1723-1777), Robert (1725-1752) and Joseph (1732-1794), were at times during the 1750s in Henrico County, Virginia, a state where they bought land, presumably for tobacco growing. Emmanuel, meanwhile, had in that decade formed a partnership with his brother Samuel (1726-1797), exporting woollen goods and worsteds to America, trading especially with Philadelphia Quaker merchants. Emmanuel was based in Philadelphia from 1760 to 1763. By the 1770s they were exporting cloth throughout North America: the American war of independence, however, led to the collapse of the market, and cloth piled high in the cloth halls. Nevertheless, Emmanuel, when he retired, had amassed a fortune of £200,000. The family, which between 1780 and 1810 was concerned not only in exporting cloth but in ship owning, land speculation, and banking, rapidly fell from prominence after the virtual bankruptcy of Gervase Elam's grandson Samuel (1773-1811) in 1810. *Panel D6*

Ellis, Rowland (1650-1731) and his wife Marged lived at Bryn-mawr, one of the five main Quaker houses near Dolgellau, Merioneth. He became a convinced Quaker in 1672, and in 1676 was among the Dolgellau Friends tried at Bala before Judge Walcot for not attending church and for refusing to take the oath. In 1686 he and many others emigrated to Pennsylvania: he returned to Wales, but in 1697 settled at Plymouth, Pennsylvania, with his family. He was a member of the Pennsylvania Assembly. The pioneer American college for women, Bryn Mawr (1885), stands on part of the estate he once owned. *Panel F13*

Ellwood, Thomas (1639-1713), the youngest son of an Oxfordshire squire of parliamentary sympathies, was thrown into the company of his father's friends Isaac and Mary Penington *qqv* of Chalfont St Peter. He first went to a Quaker meeting in December 1659 and was influenced by Edward Burrough *qv* and James Nayler. He settled at Hunger Hill, near Jordans, and in 1669 married Mary Ellis. In 1662 he had formed a friendship with John Milton and, by a chance remark, prompted his writing of *Paradise regained* (1671). His *History of the life of Thomas Ellwood* (1714) is a lively autobiography and he undertook the laborious task of editing George Fox's *Journal* (1694). *Panel C8*

Fell, Thomas (1598-1658), puritan judge, was the owner of Swarthmoor Hall, near Ulverston, in the Furness district of Lancashire. He married in 1632 Margaret Askew (1614-1702, who married George Fox *qv* in 1669). He never threw in his lot with Quakers, but his supportiveness, which included allowing meetings for worship in his home and its development as an administrative and pastoral centre, was a significant fact in the development of the infant movement. *Panel C1*

Fisher, Mary (1623?-1698), a Yorkshire servant girl, was an early convert to Quakerism and was imprisoned in York in 1652 for 16 months for 'declaring truth in the steeplehouse' at Selby. It was in prison that she learned to write. At the end of December 1653 she and Elizabeth Williams, 20 years her senior, arrived in Cambridge where, as a result of their efforts to give the Quaker message, they were publicly scourged and imprisoned. The following year she was again imprisoned at York, this time for 12 weeks. In late 1655 she travelled with Ann Austin *qv* to Barbados and New England (*see Ann Austin entry for details*). In 1662 she married William Bayly (d.1675), a Dorset mariner; she subsequently remarried and emigrated to Charleston, South Carolina. *Panel B2*

Fothergill, John (1712-1780) was the son of a Quaker Wensleydale farmer. After studying medicine at Edinburgh University he set up practice in London in 1740. While initially prescribing the reputed specifics for various disorders he came to put increasing stress on diet and regular habits of life, including fresh air and exercise. He acquired considerable wealth from his practice but continued to live simply. In 1762 he bought a 30-acre estate at Upton, Essex, for development as a botanical garden. He had met Peter Collinson *qv* soon after coming to London and through him was put in touch with John Bartram *qv*, exchanging plants with him and other collectors. He was elected a fellow of the Royal Society in 1763. He and William Tuke *qv* were among the group of Friends who secured the establishment of Ackworth School (1779). *Panels D8, D9*

Fowler, Robert, of Bridlington, Yorkshire, was convinced in 1652 by the ministry of William Dewsbury (1621-1688).

The narrative of the 1657 voyage of the *Woodhouse* was published as *A Quaker's sea-journal* (1659). He has sometimes been erroneously identified with the Robert Fowler (d.1667) who was, however, a Lincolnshire Friend. *Panel A5*

Fox, George (1624-1691) was the son of Christopher and Mary (Lago) Fox, his father being a weaver and his mother 'of the stock of the martyrs'. Besides journeys in Britain he was in Ireland (1669), the West Indies and North America (1671-3) and in Holland and Germany (1677, 1684). He was eight times imprisoned – Nottingham (1649), Derby (1650-1), Carlisle (1653), Launceston (1656), Lancaster (1660), Leicester (1662), Lancaster and Scarborough (1664-6), Worcester (1673-5). During the last of these he dictated his *Journal* which, edited by Thomas Ellwood *qv* (1694), became a spiritual classic. He wrote or dictated some 250 tracts, many of which were collected in *Gospel truth demonstrated* (1706) while his many pastoral letters were published as *A collection of epistles* (1698). *Panels A1, B1, D1, E1, F1; quotations also at B7, C1, C2, C7, D3*

Garrett, Thomas (1789-1871), who was born at Upper Darby, Pennsylvania, moved in the early 1820s to Wilmington, Delaware, where he became a substantial merchant. He made his home, 227 Shipley Street, a 'station' on the 'Underground Railroad' and is known to have helped some 2,700 slaves to freedom. In 1848 he was convicted of aiding escaping slaves and was fined £5,400, his personal property being distrained to pay the fine. This, however, only led him to redouble his efforts. *Panel F10*

Gurney, John II (1688-1741), the son of a Norwich wool merchant who had become a Quaker in 1683, became a partner in the business with his brother Joseph (1692-1750). In 1720 he was examined before the House of Lords in relation to the prohibition of the import of calico and cotton manufactures and stated so lucidly and eloquently the case of the woollen manufacturers, and the threat to them of such imports, that the successful outcome was largely attributed to him and he became known as 'the weavers' friend'. *Panel D6*

Hanbury, sir Thomas (1832-1907) did not follow his father and grandfather in the pharmaceutical business of Allen & Hanbury (*panel E12*) but founded at Shanghai (1853) Hanbury & Co, silk merchants. He bought in 1867 La Mortola, Liguria, Italy, whose garden became famous. He also enabled the Royal Horticultural Society to acquire its site at Wisley. *Panel D8*

Hodgkin, Thomas (1798-1866) qualified in medicine at Edinburgh. After two years in Paris he became in 1825 physician to the London Dispensary (1777) in Spitalfields and secured a number of appointments at Guy's Hospital. The description 'Hodgkin's disease' was later given to his discoveries set out in 'On some morbid appearances of the adsorbent glands and spleen' (1832). As early as 1818 he described the plight of aborigines following the settlement of lands by Europeans, and his criticisms in the 1830s of the activities of the Hudson's Bay Company led to a rupture with the committee of Guy's Hospital and in 1837 to his resignation. That year he was active in establishing the Aborigines Protection Society and he edited *The colonial intelligencer and aborigines friend* from 1847 to 1856. *Panel D9*

Hooton, Elizabeth (1600?-1672) of Ollerton, Nottinghamshire, became a member of a separatist group in Mansfield and was in 1647 one of the first to accept the message of George Fox *qv*: between then and 1655 she was four times imprisoned (Derby; York; Lincoln, twice). In 1661, shortly after the execution of Mary Dyer *qv* and other Friends, she and another woman Friend sailed for Massachusetts: they were immediately imprisoned and, on release, driven from the colony, eventually reaching tolerant Rhode Island, whence they sailed for the West Indies. They returned to Boston to testify against the spirit of persecution but were sent away by the same ship, landing in Virginia, whence they took passage for England. She was among the group who in 1671 accompanied George Fox on his first visit to the Americas: they came by way of Barbados and Jamaica, but she died shortly after reaching the mainland. *Panel B2*

Howgill, Francis (1618-1669), who farmed near Grayrigg, Westmorland, was one of the leaders of the seeker groups of that county, centred on the Sedbergh-Preston Patrick area. He, with a substantial number of the group, was convinced in 1652 by the message of George Fox *qv*. He was imprisoned at Appleby that year and in 1654, with his friend Edward Burrough *qv*, began preaching the Quaker message in London. They both travelled extensively in Ireland in 1655. He was author or co-author of some 40 tracts and was for the last five years of his life prisoner in Newgate. *Panels C5, C9*

Hustler, John (1715-1790), a Bradford wool-stapler, moved there about 1740 and 'soon became one of the town's leading citizens, figuring in parliamentary enquiries and petitions, helping to establish turnpike trusts, becoming chairman and treasurer of an association of worsted manufacturers, being instrumental in creating the Worsted Committee, founding the Bradford Piece Hall in 1773 and becoming a director of the Bradford Banking Company' (David James, *Bradford*, 1990). He bought a 90-acre estate at Undercliffe and built his house there. In 1768 he joined in the promotion of a cross-Pennine canal, authorised by the Leeds & Liverpool Canal Act 1770: he was treasurer until his death and, in the last year of his life, attended parliament to urge upon MPs a bill to authorise an important modification in the route. He took an active part in the founding of Ackworth School (*panel C7*). His son John (1768-1842) successfully continued the business, buying Undercliffe for £12,000 after his elder brother's death in 1802. He was one of the founders with Joseph Rowntree and Samuel Tuke *qqv* of the Friends Provident Institution (1832) (*panel E11*), being a director and treasurer until his death. *Panel D6*

Lawson, Thomas (1630-1691) was born at Clapham, west Yorkshire, and after education at Giggleswick School and Cambridge University, became minister (perhaps

unordained) at Rampside, in the Furness district of Lancashire: in 1652 he invited George Fox *qv* to preach and, convinced by what he heard, became a Quaker. After travelling in Sussex with the Quaker message he married in 1659 Frances Wilkinson of Great Strickland, Westmorland, where he was schoolmaster until 1671. His interest in botany appears to have been awakened by John Ray's *Catalogus plantarum Angliae* (1670): for the remaining 20 years of his life he was, in Ray's words, a 'diligent, industrious and skilful botanist'. Assertions that he was a herbalist or practised medicine must, however, be treated with great caution. *Panel D8*

Lettsom, John Coakley (1744-1815) was born of Quaker parents in Tortola, Virgin Islands, West Indies. He was educated in England and apprenticed to Abraham Sutcliffe (1721-1798), a Settle apothecary. He then went to London where John Fothergill *qv* advised him on his further studies, and he became a friend of Peter Collinson *qv*. In 1768, after a year in Tortola winding up the family estate, he began medical studies at Edinburgh, later travelling extensively on the continent, visiting medical schools. His concern for the medical care of the poor led him to establish the Aldersgate Dispensary. He was also active in the founding of the Medical Society of London (1773), Royal Humane Society (1774) and Royal Sea-Bathing Infirmary, Margate (1791). In 1779 he built a house at The Grove, Camberwell, and by 1795 had 10 acres of garden for his botanical specimens. He was elected a fellow of the Royal Society in 1773. *Panel D8*

Lister, Joseph (1827-1912), *baron Lister*, was the son of Joseph Jackson Lister (1786-1869), a Quaker wine merchant and friend of Thomas Hodgkin *qv*. J J L had a passion for optical instruments and was a founder member of the Microscopical Society. His researches on the nature of red corpuscles in mammalian blood give him a significant place in medicine in his own right: he was elected a fellow of the Royal Society in 1832. The son is best known as the founder of antiseptic surgery and, though he left Friends at the time of his marriage in 1856 (and was perhaps increasingly distancing himself from formal association before that), he remained, in the words of Alfred Salter *qv* 'a man of simple habits – extremely modest and forgetful of himself, with a devotion to truth, a passionate love for humanity, and a remarkable serenity of character'. He was elected a fellow of the Royal Society in 1860. *Panel D9*

Lonsdale, Kathleen (1903-1971), crystallographer, made her first major contribution to the subject in 1924 in a paper in the Royal Society's *Philosophical transactions*. In 1927 she married Thomas Lonsdale (1902?-1979) and in 1935 they joined the Society of Friends at Uxbridge. In 1938 she began to take an interest in both static and dynamic disorders in crystals and in 1946 became reader in crystallography at University College, London. She was the author of *Crystals and X-rays* (1948). She was elected a fellow of the Royal Society in 1945 (one of the first two women) and in 1968 was the first woman president of the British Association. During the second world war, unable to make a witness against conscription in any other way, she refused to register for firewatching (which she was doing voluntarily) and, refusing on principle to pay the fine, was imprisoned in Holloway: this led to a continuing concern for penal reform. She gave much time to peace and international issues – she was a member of a Quaker delegation to Russia in 1951 and edited the report *Quakers visit Russia*; she wrote a Penguin Special *Is peace possible?* (1957); and she was president of the British Section of the Women's International League for Peace & Freedom. *Panel D 10*

Maddock, James (1715?-1786), a Warrington soap-boiler, moved after his marriage to Yarmouth, Norfolk, and in 1776 to London, setting up as a florist and establishing the Walworth Nursery, which appears to be the first in the London area to issue priced catalogues, hitherto a distinctively northern practice. His son **James (1763-1825)**, who married in 1788 Mary Curtis of Alton, niece of William Curtis *qv*, had entered the business. He published his father's *Florist's directory, or a treatise on the culture of flowers* (1792) and in 1798 moved with his family to Alton, his wife's younger brother Samuel Curtis later taking over the Walworth Nursery. *Panel D 8*

May, Charles (1801-1860) came, on his father's side, from a line of clockmakers at Witney and Henley-on-Thames, Oxfordshire, and, on his mother's, from a line of apothecaries and botanists (William Curtis *qv* was her first cousin). In 1836 he joined James Ransome *qv* of Ipswich, substantially developing the firm's railway work, and concentrating on chairs and fastenings in rail laying, for which a patent was taken out in 1841. He left the firm about 1851 and took up instrument making, Greenwich Observatory being among his customers. He was elected a fellow of the Royal Society in 1854. *Panel D 7*

Meade, William (1628-1713), a member of an Essex landowning family, had settled in London, becoming a wealthy linen-draper. In 1670, the year of his trial alongside William Penn *qv*, he purchased the estate of Gooses (Gesyns), near Romford, Essex. He was active in Quaker administration and in 1677 was briefly responsible for financial management of the fund for employing poor Friends in spinning (a responsibility later undertaken by John Bellers *qv*). In 1681 he married, as his second wife, Sarah, daughter of Thomas Fell *qv*. In 1669 Thomas Fell's widow married George Fox *qv* who, when in London, frequently stayed with his son-in-law at Gooses. Meade was a man of strong opinions and quick decisions and in the last decade of the century a firm adherent of the Whig principles of the Revolution: this brought him into political, and more general, conflict with Penn. *Panel F 2*

Mott, Lucretia (1793-1880), born into a Nantucket Quaker family, was married in 1811 to James Mott (1788-1868): they settled shortly afterwards in Philadelphia. She was one of the founders of the Philadelphia Female Anti-slavery Society (1833) and followed William Lloyd Garrison (1805-1879) in urging 'immediate and unconditional' abolition as against the 'gradualism' approach of most American and British Quakers. For these and theological reasons she was not a welcome delegate to the London World Anti-slavery Convention

(1840) and was, as a woman, excluded from the floor. This episode led directly to the first feminist conference at Seneca Falls, NY, in 1848. *Panel F 10*

Newman, sir George (1870-1948), pioneer in public and child health, was the son of Henry Stanley Newman (1837-1912), a Leominster grocer who was active in Quaker evangelistic and missionary work and editor of *The Friend* from 1892 to 1912. The son qualified as a doctor in 1892, becoming medical officer of health for Finsbury in 1900, chief medical officer for the School Medical Service in 1907, and, in addition, chief medical officer to the Ministry of Health in 1919. He was chairman of the Friends Ambulance Unit (*panel F 8*) from 1914 to 1919. His books include *Infant mortality* (1906) and *The building of a nation's health* (1939) and through his annual reports to the Ministry he had an enduring influence on public health. *Panel D 9*

Nicholas I (1796-1855), emperor of Russia 1825-55, was the brother of Alexander I *qv* but, despite reverence for his brother's memory, he reversed what liberal policies there had been in the earlier reign. He continued interest in Daniel Wheeler's work, however, and provided a handsome burial ground for Wheeler's wife and daughter (*panel F 4*), who both died in Russia. *Panel F 5*

Oliver, Daniel (1830-1916) was born of Quaker parents at Newcastle upon Tyne and in his youth was a prominent member of that meeting's Askensian Society, whose members gave fortnightly lectures on scientific subjects. Botany gradually ousted mineralogy as his main interest. In 1858 he became librarian of the Kew Herbarium and in 1861 professor of botany at University College, London. He became a fellow of the Royal Society in 1863 and was appointed keeper of the Kew Herbarium the following year. He retired from official life in 1890. *Panel D 8*

Parkinson, Sydney (1745?-1771), son of a Quaker brewer in Edinburgh, was put to the business of a woollen-draper in London. His pleasure and proficiency in drawing flowers and fruits attracted the notice of botanists: he was recommended to Joseph Banks as a botanical and zoological draughtsman and was chosen to go to the South Seas with Captain Cook on the *Endeavour*. He died in the course of the voyage but his work was published as *A journal of a voyage to the South Seas* (1773), reissued under the editorship of John Coakley Lettsom *qv* in 1784. *Panel D 8*

Pease, Edward (1767-1858) was the son of a Darlington Quaker woolcomber and joined the family business. From the early nineteenth century he was preoccupied with securing effective transport to the coast. Plans launched in 1810 for a canal did not prosper and from 1818 (by which time the family also had colliery interests) he was one of a group campaigning for a rail or waggon way. It was George Stephenson (1781-1848) who converted him to the idea of steam locomotives. *Panel D 7*

Pease, Henry (1807-1881) was the youngest of the eight children of Edward Pease *qv*. His brother Joseph (1799-1872) was the first Quaker to enter parliament and was member for South Durham 1833-41, a constituency

Henry represented 1857-65. The two brothers had expanded the family's railway and colliery interests, acquired ironstone mines, and in effect founded the town of Middlesbrough. Both brothers had been successively president of the Peace Society. *Panel F5*

Penington, Isaac (1616-1679), whose father was lord mayor of London 1642-3 and a representative of the city in the Long Parliament, married in 1654 **Mary (1625-1682)**, widow of Sir William Springett: they settled at Chalfont St Peter and later at Amersham, Buckinghamshire. Mary Penington's daughter, Gulielma Maria Springett, became the wife of William Penn *qv*. The Peningtons first attended a Quaker meeting in 1656, becoming decided Friends two years later. Isaac Penington, who suffered five imprisonments, was a voluminous author and letter writer. *Panel B4*

Penn, William (1644-1718), son of Admiral Sir William Penn (1621-1670), was brought up in London and Ireland, where he was in 1667 convinced of Quaker principles by the preaching of the Oxford tradesman Thomas Loe (d. 1668). He married in 1672 Gulielma Maria Springett (1644-1694), daughter of Mary and step-daughter of Isaac Penington *qqv*. He twice visited Pennsylvania in person (1682-4, 1699-1701). He had married in 1696 Hannah Callowhill (1671-1726) who accompanied him on the second visit. He was a prolific author, having written over 100 books and tracts. *Panels D7, F2, F11*

Pius VII (1740-1823), pope 1800-23, had been prisoner of the invading French troops 1809-14. On 9 December 1819 he received Stephen Grellet in private audience (longer than was customary): they covered much ground – prisons and reformatories, the inquisition, the nature of the church and the grounds of gospel ministry. *Panel B5*

90

Quare, Daniel (1648-1724) was admitted a brother of the Clock Makers Company in 1671, becoming warden 1705-7 and master in 1708. He invented and made a repeating movement for watches and in 1680 perfected his design. In 1695 he turned his attention to barometers, bringing out a portable one which was unspillable. He declined on conscientious grounds when William III wished to appoint him as the king's watchmaker. He was an active member of Meeting for Sufferings (*panel A3*) and was largely responsible for the work of its Parliamentary Committee. His daughter married Silvanus Bevan (1691-1765), an apothecary whose premises in Plough Court were later to be the headquarters of William Allen. *Panel D5*

Ransome, James (1782-1849) was the son of Robert Ransome (1753-1830), a Quaker ironmaster from Norwich who in 1789 started a foundry in Ipswich, in 1803 patented an improved ploughshare, and in 1808 a method of interchangeable ploughshares. In 1809 James joined the firm and started diversification into general civil engineering, including bridge building and, later, the provision of Ipswich's gas supply. Some early railway work was undertaken and when Charles May *qv* joined the firm in 1836 this was considerably expanded. From 1846 to 1852 the firm was styled Ransomes & May. The balance sheet for 1851 valued agricultural work at £35,000 but railway and other work at £87,000. *Panel D7*

Reynolds, Richard (1735-1816) was born of Quaker parents in Bristol, his great grandfather, Michael, of Faringdon, Berkshire, having been convinced by the preaching of George Fox *qv*. He was apprenticed to a Bristol grocer and soon after his apprenticeship ended he was sent to Coalbrookdale on business and met and in 1757 married Hannah Darby, daughter of Abraham II *qv*. She died in 1762 and his father-in-law the following year. During RR's management of the works he made a great advance in the use of waggon ways. He was also concerned over river transport: Severn barges were pulled by men who had to scramble along the precipitous and rocky banks of the river, and in 1772 Reynolds pressed unsuccessfully for legislation for a towpath. In 1804 he retired and returned to Bristol. *Panel D4*

Reynolds, William (1758-1803), son of Richard Reynolds *qv*, devoted himself at an early age to scientific studies and in his late teens was given a share of responsibility for the Ketley forge and works. By this time his admiration for the work of James Watt (1736-1819) heralded a 20-year era of co-operation between the Coalbrookdale Company and Boulton & Watt. WR was responsible for the 2-mile towpath between Coalport and the Iron Bridge, was substantially the designer of the 'upper canal' at Coalbrookdale, and also the 1788 inclined plane which connected it by a drop of 73 feet to the 'lower canal', level with the Ketley ironworks. *Panel D4*

Rotch, William (1734-1828) was the head of the family conducting the Quaker whale fishery in Nantucket. Following the war of independence a number of Quaker whalers, Rotch among them, settled in 1785 at Dunkirk. He returned to America in 1794, settling at New Bedford, Massachusetts. His son Benjamin, however, that year moved to Milford Haven, joining a number of his fellow-Quakers who had settled there in 1792. *Panel F12*

Rowntree, John Wilhelm (1868-1905), son of Joseph Rowntree II *qv*, entered his father's factory at 17 and was responsible two years later for reorganising the cocoa and chocolate department. Though disciplining himself to take his full share in the business, he did not warm to it, having greater artistic gifts and a passion for the theatre. He took a full part in adult school work as a teacher and, with Henry Bryan Binns (1873-1923), wrote *A history of the adult school movement* (1903). As a result of the Manchester Conference (1895) he founded and edited the periodical *Present day papers* (1899-1902) and was active in the summer school movement for Biblical and social study and in the foundation of Woodbrooke (*panel B6*). He had suffered from deafness since his teens and in 1894, on *Retinitis pigmentosa* being diagnosed, he was warned of impending and irreparable blindness. In 1899 he retired to Scalby, near Scarborough and devoted himself to Quaker and adult school work, planning a comprehensive history of Quakerism which was written by others after his early death. *Panels A8, D11*

Rowntree, Joseph I (1801-1859), son of John and Elizabeth (Lotherington) Rowntree of Scarborough, moved to York in 1822, opening a successful grocery business in Pavement. He took a substantial part in civic life and in Quaker concerns and was an amateur statistician of no mean order. His concern for education found expression in his membership of the Ackworth School Committee (1827-59) and his substantial part in founding the Friends Educational Society (1837): in these and many other matters he worked closely with Samuel Tuke *qv*. *Panel E11*

Rowntree, Joseph II (1836-1925), son of Joseph Rowntree I *qv*, was apprenticed to his father and entered his grocery business in Pavement, York. His brother Henry Isaac Rowntree (1838-1883) had in 1860 joined, and two years later bought, the York cocoa, chocolate and chicory business previously in the hands of the Tuke family *qv* (the tea firm had been separated and moved to London): in 1869 Joseph joined his brother at the Tanners Moat factory, whose main standby was then fruit gums. There were then 14 employees and he lived to see the firm grow to over 7,000. He was a regular adult school teacher for most of his life. He was radical in outlook and when, in 1904, he established his three trusts, he noted in his memorandum that 'Much of our philanthropic effort is directed to remedying the more superficial manifestations of weakness or evil, while little thought is directed to search out their underlying causes' and expressed the hope that his trustees would concentrate on the latter. *Panels D11, E7*

Salter, Alfred (1873-1945) was inspired as a medical student by Lister's battle against gangrene. Learning that Joseph Lister *qv* had been brought up a Quaker he became interested, joining the Society of Friends in 1900: the same year he married Ada Brown (1867-1942), who was to share his life's work. From 1897 to 1900 he had been bacteriologist at the Lister Institute (invited by Lister himself) but increasingly he saw his future work as among the slum dwellers of Bermondsey. Seeing a vacant corner shop, he rented it as his surgery, but, recognising that medical treatment could do little when housing conditions were so bad, he joined the borough council in 1903 and campaigned successfully not only for a vigorous policy of house building but also for trees in every street and flowers in every open space. Ada Salter, who was an equal in these campaigns, was, as mayor of Bermondsey in 1922, the first woman mayor in London. *Panel D9*

Scott, Job (1751-1793), who was born at Providence, Rhode Island, was a man of deep spiritual experience and a ministering Friend in the mystical tradition. He published only one work, *The baptism of Christ a gospel ordinance, being altogether inward and spiritual* (1793) but his *Journal* (1797) was frequently reprinted and influential. He travelled extensively in the ministry and died at Ballitore, Co. Kildare, Ireland. *Panel B4*

Singleton, William (1770?-1832), schoolmaster, left the Methodist New Connexion and joined Friends about 1800, soon after starting the Nottingham adult school. He was reading master at Ackworth School from 1807 to 1812 when he started his own school at Loxley, near Sheffield:

the sons of Daniel Wheeler *qv* were among his pupils. He was a staunch opposer of corporal punishment. He was in the Gambia in 1821 on an exploratory visit for the projected educational and linguistic work of Hannah Kilham (1774-1832). He returned by the end of the year for the marriage of his daughter Anne (1798?-1863) to George Edmondson *qv*. Singleton had been getting increasingly at cross-purposes with Sheffield Quakers and resigned his membership in 1823. *Panel E7*

Still, William (1821-1902), freeborn negro, was from 1847 until about 1861 a clerk in the Pennsylvania Society for the Abolition of Slavery. He was active in his work for runaway slaves and his *The Underground Railroad* (1872) remains one of the best accounts of the operation. *Panel F10*

Sturge, Joseph (1793-1859), the son of a Quaker farmer in Gloucestershire, became a corn factor in Birmingham. The company grew into one of the largest grain importers in Britain and made important investments in the Gloucester docks and in the Birmingham & Gloucester Railway. From about 1825 he was active in the anti-slavery movement and, after the Emancipation Act 1833, he campaigned against the apprenticeship system of unpaid labour which the act provided for. Following a personal visit with Thomas Harvey (1812-1884) they published *The West Indies in 1837* (1838). In the 1840s he was prominent in the Anti-Corn Law League and the National Complete Suffrage Union, though in the latter case failing to hold together the moderates and the chartists. Following his 1854 visit to Russia with Robert Charleton and Henry Pease *qqv* he went to Finland in 1856 with Thomas Harvey to promote relief efforts following devastation of the fishing fleets during the Crimean war. *Panels E7, F5*

Thompson, Frances (1840-1926) was born in Liverpool and came of a family of Quaker pharmacists who were devoted to art and literature more than was common among Friends at that time. She moved to Birkenhead in 1895 and was closely associated with her friend Ellen Robinson (1840-1912) in work for peace. Together they founded the Liverpool & Birkenhead Women's Peace & Arbitration Society. She also lectured on social and literary subjects. She was anxious that Quakers should get to grips with scientific thought and the textual criticism of the Bible and was a warm supporter of John Wilhelm Rowntree *qv* in the summer school movement. *Panel A8*

Tubman, Harriet (1821?-1913), fugitive slave and a leading figure in the 'Underground Railroad', made a score of journeys into the south, escorting some 300 fugitive slaves to freedom. Her 1869 memoirs were reissued as *Harriet the Moses of her people* (1886). *Panel F10*

Tuke, Samuel (1784-1857) was a grandson of William Tuke *qv*: he continued in the family business as tea dealers and chocolate and cocoa manufacturers and was active in expanding it. He was, however, extremely active outside business. His educational interests found expression in his membership of the Ackworth School Committee (1812-51) and his substantial share in the founding of Lawrence Street (later Bootham) and The Mount Schools, York, and of the Friends Educational Society (1837): in all these and many other matters he worked closely with Joseph Rowntree *qv*. He was the author of *Description of The Retreat* (1813) and he was active in the anti-slavery movement. He was clerk of the yearly meeting of British Quakers 1832-7. *Panel E11*

Tuke, William (1733-1822) inherited the York grocery business of his formidable aunt Mary Tuke (1695-1752): he specialised as a tea dealer and before he retired as a partner in 1818 chocolate and cocoa manufacture had been added. He married in 1754 Elizabeth Hoyland (1729?-1760) and it was after her death that he began to take an interest in Quaker affairs. In 1765 he married Esther Maud (1727?-1794). He was, with John Fothergill *qv* and others, closely involved in the foundation of Ackworth School (1779) and as a result of his wife's initiative a school for girls was opened in Trinity Lane, York (1784), a forerunner of The Mount. It was as a result of his efforts that Yorkshire Quakers in 1792 approved the establishment of 'A Friends Institute for the Mentally Afflicted': The Retreat, York, was opened on 11 May 1796. *Panel D9*

Walker, George Washington (1800-1859) was born in London of Unitarian parents. He was apprenticed to Quaker drapers at Newcastle upon Tyne and joined Friends in 1827. He accompanied James Backhouse *qv* in visiting Tasmania, parts of mainland Australia, Mauritius and South Africa between 1831 and 1840. He then returned to Tasmania and married Sarah Benson Mather, settling in Hobart Town where he ran a linen-drapery and haberdashery business. *Panel F20*

Westwood, Mary (d. 1667) has long remained a shadowy figure, for whom nearly 60 pamphlets were printed between 1659 and 1665. There is, however, strong probability that she is to be identified with the Mary Westwood who died in January 1667 and whose body was interred in Friends' burial ground, Bunhill Fields. She appears to have acted as editor, guide and publisher mainly to Friends unused to having their work printed: of 15 'infrequent' authors for whom she acted (often Friends outside London), 11 had their first work published by her. She appears to have employed a printer with a very limited range of type at his disposal (and that old and battered) and whose setting and printing were done by a not very competent journeyman or an apprentice. The body of work she published is important because it illustrates a level in publishing and distribution quite different from the mainstream Quaker, or other radical, printers and publishers. *Panel B4*

Wheeler, Daniel (1771-1840) was born in London, orphaned at an early age, and went to sea. After serving in the British army and navy he resigned his commission, settling in Yorkshire with his sister, who had become a Quaker. In 1799, in Sheffield, he too joined Friends and his gift in the vocal ministry was acknowledged soon after. He became a successful seed merchant and farmer. After his years in Russia (1818-32) and the South Seas (1833-8) he twice visited America. He died in New York. *Panel F4*

White, William (1820-1900) was born in Reading and brought up a Wesleyan. In 1841 George Palmer (1818-1897) came to the town: he and his brother William Isaac Palmer (1824-1893) became White's lifelong friends in temperance and Sunday School work. In 1843 he went to Burton-on-Trent and in 1846 to Brighton and during these years, following the Palmer contacts, he became a Quaker. In 1848 he and Cornelius Pike (1826?-1869) established a printing business in Birmingham. Here White was immediately drawn into work for adult schools which quickened his understanding of housing conditions. He joined the town council in 1873 and was soon appointed chairman of a committee charged with clearing the worst slum property in the centre of the town. He was mayor in 1882. *Panel E7*

Whittier, John Greenleaf (1807-1892), poet and abolitionist, was born at Haverhill, Massachusetts, the son of a Quaker farmer. He extended his limited formal education by wide reading. Converted to abolitionism in 1833, he devoted himself for 30 years to the anti-slavery cause, both as poet and lobbyist. He edited from 1838 to 1840 the *Pennsylvania freeman*. When the American Anti-slavery Society split in 1840, Whittier sided with the 'gradualists' as against the 'immediates' led by William Lloyd Garrison (1805-1879). Whittier was more and more turning to pure literature and in middle and later life volumes of prose and poetry poured from his pen. His edition of *The journal of John Woolman* (1871) represents a significant step in the revival of interest in Woolman's message. *Panel E12*

Wilkinson, John (1728-1808) was a notable ironmaster who had several business connections with Friends. A Cumberland man, he moved to Staffordshire about 1748 and subsequently to Bersham, near Wrexham. In the early 1760s he also established himself at Broseley, on the opposite side of the Severn from Coalbrookdale. He and Abraham Darby III *qv* together planned the iron bridge which was opened in 1781, Wilkinson's involvement being both financial and technical. Though probably an Anglican at least nominally, Wilkinson was locally regarded as an atheist and, from the 1790s, as a disciple of Thomas Paine (1737-1809). *Panels D4, D7*

Worsdell, Thomas Clarke (1788-1862), coachbuilder, after apprenticeship in London moved between 1812 and 1816 to Lancashire where he and his wife joined Friends. In 1827 the family settled in Liverpool and the following year he and his son Nathaniel (1809-1886) were invited to tea by George Stephenson (1781-1848) to discuss designs for coaches on the Liverpool & Manchester Railway. TCW soon became superintendent of coaching for that company and many of his descendants became notable railway engineers. *Panel D7*

Appendix B: Arrangement of panels

As explained in the introduction, panels were arranged in groups relating to a chapter or chapters in *Christian faith and practice* as approved by the Yearly Meeting of British Quakers in 1959. The titles of these chapters are given here, together with a list of panels in each group.

The title panel (The prism) was based on the preamble to chapter 1 (Spiritual experiences of Friends)

Section A (God and man) was based on the following chapters: 1 (Spiritual experiences of Friends), 2 (God and man), 3 (Friends and the Christian church):

A1 George Fox's convincement
A2 James Nayler
A3 James Parnell; Meeting for Sufferings
A4 Richard Seller
A5 Voyage of the *Woodhouse*
A6 John Woolman
A7 Conscientious objection
A8 Manchester Conference 1895
A9 Oaths

Section B (Publishing truth) was based on chapter 8 (Publishing truth):

B1 Firbank Fell: George Fox preaching
B2 Mary Fisher
B3 John Bright
B4 Publishers of Truth
B5 Stephen Grellet
B6 Woodbrooke
B7 Service overseas
B8 Quaker Peace Action Caravan

Section C (The meeting) was based on the following chapters: 4 (The meeting for worship), 5 (Vocal ministry), 6 (Retirement and prayer), 7 (The meeting as a fellowship), 15 (The world family of Friends):

C1 Swarthmoor Hall
C2 Margaret Fell
C3 Keeping the meeting
C4 Meeting houses
C5 Meeting houses overseas
C6 Meeting houses in the community
C7 Schools
C8 Marriage
C9 Pilgrimages
C10 Children and young people
C11 Leaveners

Section D (The art of living) was based on the following chapters: 9 (The art of living), 10 (Marriage and the home), 11 (Stages of life):

D1 George Fox: Lichfield, Pendle Hill
D2 Simplicity
D3 Persecution in Oxford
D4 Coalbrookdale
D5 Innocent trades
D6 Merchants
D7 Railways
D8 Botanists
D9 True health
D10 Scientists
D11 Industrial welfare
D12 Ecology
D13 Scott Bader Commonwealth

Section E (Social responsibilities) was based on chapter 12 (Social responsibilities):

E1 George Fox at Ulverston: healing
E2 John Bellers
E3 Bankering
E4 Criminal justice
E5 Elizabeth Fry
E6 Elizabeth Fry and the patchwork quilts
E7 Adult schools
E8 Ireland: The great hunger 1845-8
E9 Mary Hughes
E10 Unemployment
E11 Friends Provident Institution
E12 William Allen

Section F (National and international responsibilities) was based on the following chapters: 13 (National responsibilities), 14 (International responsibilities), 15 (The world family of Friends):

F1 George Fox in Derby gaol
F2 The Penn and Meade trial 1670
F3 The slave trade
F4 Daniel Wheeler
F5 Delegation to the Czar 1854
F6 Relief work: British Isles
F7 Relief work overseas
F8 Friends Ambulance Unit
F9 Northern Ireland: Reconciliation
F10 The Underground Railroad
F11 Penn and Pennsylvania
F12 Nantucket and Milford Haven
F13 Dolgellau and Pennsylvania
F14 New Zealand/Aotearoa
F15 Work camps
F16 Peace embassies
F17 Vigils for peace
F18 World Conference 1991
F19 South Africa
F20 Tasmania
F21 Canada
F22 The Netherlands 1940-5

The final panel (The world family of Friends) was based on chapter 15 (The world family of Friends)

Appendix C: Sources of quotations

The source of the principal quotations in the tapestry panels is given below. The panel number is followed by the first two or three words of the quotation. The standard, or most readily available, printed source is then given. Where the quotation is in *Christian faith and practice in the experience of the Society of Friends* (1960), *Church government* (1968), or *Quaker faith and practice* (1995) this is shown by *CFP*, *CG*, or *QFP* followed by the extract number. The needs of the panels sometimes precluded exact quotation and where it differs from the original, this is indicated. Quotations from *The journal of George Fox* are, unless otherwise stated, from the edition edited by John L. Nickalls (1952) and are indicated *JGF*. Quotations from the Bible give chapter and verse, separated by a colon.

Prism 'The Religious Society' *CFP*, preamble to chapter 1; *QFP* 18.20

A1 'There is one' *JGF* p.11 (entry relating to 1647); *CFP* 5; *QFP* 19.02
'A church is' slight variant of *JGF* p.107 (entry relating to 1652)

A2 'There is a' James Nayler, *To all the beloved people of God*, 1660, p.8; reprinted in his *A collection of sundry books, epistles and papers*, 1716, p.696; *CFP* 25; *QFP* 19.12

A3 'Be willing that' James Parnell, *The fruits of a fast*, 1655, p.30; reprinted in his *A collection of the several writings*, 1675, p.293
'I must see' L.Violet Hodgkin, *A book of Quaker saints*, 1917, p.257; repr. 1972, p.197

A4 'I am not free' slight variant of 'An account of the sufferings of Richard Seller', printed in Joseph Besse, *A collection of the sufferings of the people called Quakers*, 1753, vol.2, p.112
'I am at peace' slight variant of the same, p.116
'I was to die' the same, p.117

A5 'Thou has her' 'A true relation of the voyage', printed in James Bowden, *The history of the Society of Friends in America*, vol.1, 1850, p.63
'Contrary to my will' slight variant of the same, p.63
'Cut through' slight variant of the same, p.64

A7 'Be faithful to' London YM, Epistle, 1744

A8 'Friends are not bound' John Wilhelm Rowntree, 'Has Quakerism a message to the world today?' in London YM, *Report of the proceedings of the conference...in Manchester, 1895*, 1896, p.82
'God's truth is given' based on Frances Thompson, 'The Society of Friends in relation to social questions', in the same, p.143

A9 'We regard the' London YM, *Christian practice*, 1911, p.139 *CFP* 571; not in *QFP*

B1 'Keep your feet' George Fox, *A collection of ... epistles*, 1698, p.152 (Epistle 195, 1660)

B3 'Alliances are' John Bright, *Speeches*, ed. J.E.Thorold Rogers, 1868, vol.1, p.468

B4 'The principal' Robert Barclay, *Apology for the true Christian divinity*', 1676, prop.3, sect.2

B5 'Proclaim unto' Stephen Grellet, *Memoirs*, ed. Benjamin Seebohm, 1860, vol.1, p.25; 2nd ed., 1861, p.19; 3rd ed., 1862, p.19 (entry relating to 1795); *CFP* 58; not in *QFP*

B7 'Be patterns' George Fox, 'Exhortation to Friends in the ministry', 1656, printed in *JGF* p.263; *CFP* 376; *QFP* 19.32

B8 'World peace will' Motto on Quaker Peace Action Caravan

C1 'You may meet' Margaret Fox in 'The testimony of MF' in George Fox, *Journal*, 1694, p.iv; Isabel Ross, *Margaret Fell, mother of Quakerism*, 1949, p.128
'A matter of' *JGF* p.174, reading 'seventy' (entry relating to 1654); cf Fox, *Journal*, 1694, p.124, reading 'above sixty'

C2 'We are a' Margaret Fox, quoted Ross, *op.cit.* p.128; not in *CFP*; *QFP* 19.46
'Although I am' Margaret Fox, *A brief collection of remarkable passages relating to ... MF*, 1710, p.8; *CFP* 21; *QFP* 19.38

C3 'For they might' slight variant of response made by Bristol Friends to the magistrates, January 1661, printed in Joseph Besse, *A collection of the sufferings of the people called Quakers*, 1753, vol.1, p.42; quoted in L.Violet Hodgkin, *A book of Quaker saints*, 1917, p.299; repr. 1972, p.225

C4 'Come with heart' London YM, *Advices and queries*, 1964, sect.2; *CG* 702

C5 'We met together' Francis Howgill, 'Testimony... concerning Edward Burrough' in EB's collected works, *The memorable works of a son of thunder*, 1672, prelim. leaf e3; *CFP* 184; *QFP* 19.08

C7 'instruct in whatsoever things' slight variant of *JGF* p.520 (entry relating to 1668); *CFP* 438; *QFP* 23.71

C8 'Seek to know' London YM, *Advices and queries*, 1964, sect.1; *CG* 702
'Friends I take' London YM, Marriage regulations in *CFP* 906; *QFP* 16.36 (in Welsh, 16.37)
'We sensibly felt' Thomas Ellwood, *History of his life*, 1714, p.257; ed. C.G.Crump, 1900, p.160 (entry relating to 1669); *CFP* 488; *QFP* 16.02

C9 'Who knows' slight variant of Elfrida Vipont Foulds, *Let your lives speak*, (*Pendle Hill pamphlet* 71), 1953, p.9; London ed., 1954, p.9
'The Kingdom of' Francis Howgill, see C5 above

C10 'Watch with' London YM, *Advices and queries*, 1964 (sect. 3); *CG* 702

D1 'Turn from darkness' adapted from *JGF* p. 105
'Be still and' George Fox, 'Letter to the Lady Claypool', 1658, printed in *JGF* p. 346; *CFP* 303; *QFP* 2.18
'I saw an' *JGF* p. 19 (entry relating to 1647); *CFP* 7; *QFP* 19.03

D2 'that the simplicity' London YM, Epistle, 1691; *CFP* 433; *QFP* 20.28

D3 'Love, wisdom and' George Fox, *A collection of … epistles*, 1698, p. 308 (Epistle 276, 1669)

D6 'Not slothful' Romans 12:11

D7 'True godliness' William Penn, *No cross, no crown*, 2nd ed., 1682, ch. 5, sect. 12; reprinted in his *A collection of the works*, 1726, vol. 1, p. 296; 3rd ed., 1782, vol. 2, p. 53; *CFP* 395; *QFP* 23.02
'in their handiwork' Ecclesiasticus 38:34

D8 'The universe is' Sarah Martha Baker, quoted in *Annual monitor* 1918 pp. 10-1 as a recollection by her Sunday School children of her teaching

D9 'True health springs' Howard E. Collier, 'Health and healing', in John Kavanaugh (ed.), *The Quaker approach to contemporary problems*, 1952, p. 196; *CFP* 477; not in *QFP*

D10 'Live up to' Caroline Fox, *Memories of old friends*, ed. H. N. Pym, 4to ed., 1882, p. xxi; London 8vo ed., 1882, vol. 1, p. xxii; Philadelphia ed., 1882, p. xxi; London ed., 1883, p. xvii (entry relating to 1840); *CFP* 75; *QFP* 26.04
'The immensities of' London YM, Draft approved by Special YM 1959; *CFP* 146; not in *QFP*

D11 'The gospel' John Wilhelm Rowntree, 'What has Jesus to say to the state?', in *Essays and addresses*, ed. Joshua Rowntree, 1905, p. 368

D12 'Cherish the' London YM, *Advices and queries*, 1964, sect. 4; *CG* 702
'Are you concerned' London YM, *Advices and queries*, 1964, query 19; *CFP* 703

E1 'I looked at it' slight abridgment of *JGF* p. 128 (entry relating to 1652)

E2 'The poor without' John Bellers, *An essay towards the improvement of physick*, 1714, p. 37; reprinted in A. Ruth Fry, *John Bellers*, 1935, p. 124, and in George Clarke (ed.), *John Bellers, his life, times and writings*, 1987, p. 204; not in *CFP*; *QFP* 23.68

E5 'Lord I believe' Mark 9:24

E9 Quoted in Hugh S. Pyper, *Mary Hughes, a friend to all in need*, 1985, p. 12

E10 'The community is' London YM, 'A social testimony', 1945; *CFP* 545; not in *QFP*

E11 'The true concern' Roger C. Wilson, *Authority, leadership and concern*, 1949, p. 12; *CFP* 363; *QFP* 13.07

E12 'cheerful, in the light' John G. Whittier, 'First-day thoughts', written 1852, in *The writings*, 1888-9, vol. 7, p. 313; *CFP* 71; not in *QFP*

F1 'Live in the' London YM, *Advices and queries*, 1928, sect. 2; based on *JGF* p. 65 (entry relating to 1651) reprinted in *CFP* 613, *QFP* 24.01
'Deal justly' slight variant of *JGF* p. 37 (entry relating to 1649)
'I spoke to them' *JGF* p. 31
'Let your yea' James 5:12; compare *JGF* pp. 2, 38 (entries relating to 1635, 1649)
'Justice Bennet' slight variant of *JGF* p. 58 (entry relating to 1650)

F3 'God hath made' Acts 17:26

F4 'God's love enableth' Daniel Wheeler, *Memoirs*, 1842, pp. 70-1; *CFP* 56; *QFP* 2.04

F5 'O mighty prince' London YM, Address to Emperor Nicholas I of Russia, in Margaret E. Hirst, *The Quakers in peace and war*, 1923, p. 535; repr. 1972, p. 535

F6 'Our life is' Isaac Penington, Letter to Friends in Amersham, 1667, in his *Letters*, ed. John Barclay, 1828, p. 139; 3rd ed., 1844, p. 138; *CFP* 404; *QFP* 10.01

F10 'Thou shalt not' Deuteronomy 23:15

F11 'For we have' slight variant of William Penn, preface to *The frame of the government of the province of Pennsylvania*, 1682; reprinted in William Penn Tercentenary Committee, *Remember William Penn*, 1945, p. 82
'Government is' slight variant of the same; reprinted in the same, p. 80

F12 'Bring the whole' London YM, *Advices and queries*, 1964, sect. 4; *CG* 702
'When the war began' variant of William Rotch, manuscript written about 1813, printed as *Memorandum written in the eightieth year of his age*, 1916, p. 1
'Gwyn ei byd' ('Blessed is') Waldo Williams, 'Y Tangnefeddwyr' ('The peacemakers'), 1941, printed in his *Dail pren* ('Leaves of a tree'), 1956, pp. 41-2

F14 'This is our vision' Slight variant from Aotearoa/New Zealand YM, 'Public statement – January 1987' as printed in London YM, *Proceedings*, 1987, pp. 210-11 and, in part, in *QFP* 24.10

F16 'True peace cannot' London YM, 'To all men everywhere', 1943; *CFP* 621; *QFP* 24.09

F17 'We utterly deny' 'A declaration from the harmless and innocent people of God called Quakers', 1661, printed in *JFG* pp. 399-400; *CFP* 614; *QFP* 24.04

WFF 'Walk cheerfully' George Fox, 'Exhortation to Friends in the ministry', 1656, printed in *JFG* p. 263; *CFP* 376; *QFP* 19.32

Index of titles of panels